The Edge of
Dawn

When No One Cared, I Did!

BRETT

Authorunit
Number and Address
877-826-5888
17130 Van Buren Blvd., Ste. 238, Riverside, CA 92504

Because of the dynamic nature of the Internet, any web addresses or links contained in this book may have changed since publication and may no longer be valid. The views expressed in this work are solely those of the author and do not necessarily reflect the views of the publisher, and the publisher hereby disclaims any responsibility for them.

ISBN: 978-1-960075-26-0 (Paperback Edition)
ISBN: 978-1-960075-27-7 (E-book Edition)

Printed in the United States.

CONTENTS

CHAPTER 1

It was 1957/1960. I remember someone carrying me to a house on Green Street between Bold Street and Mill Avenue in a small town in Maine, and I can't remember anymore.

In 1962, I lived at 922 Wayne Street in Maine with my brothers, my sister, and my mother. Growing up, I was somewhat normal as a little boy.

Then in 1963, my brother Ray set my back on fire. My other brother, Joe, put the fire out. My mother took me to a children's hospital where they put a big bandage on my back. I was in recovery for years. Then in 1964, my mother had a babysitter. We went there when she went to work. My brothers were playing with the stove, and the lady came in the kitchen and saw that the stove was on. She asked us who was playing with the stove. My brothers said that it was me playing with the stove, but I wasn't playing with the stove! The lady grabbed my hand and held it over the stove and then turned the fire on and held my hand over the fire! My fingers were burned up, and I can't remember any more after that.

Back then, we always had a lot of snow, up to our knees, when we were growing up. The coal truck came and left coal to warm our house, and the milkmen brought milk, cheese, and eggs to our house. It was great growing up back there on Wayne Street in Maine. You had all the stores there. Bays where we got our donuts. It was fun! Mom shopped at Paul's Market and the Meat Market. We ate at Keith's Restaurant and the Peak Restaurant and watched the old people drink wine and beer and shoot dice.

I went to school at Park, from first grade to fourth grade, then went to Bay Elementary from fifth grade to sixth grade. We ate at Cooks and ate Coney's dog. That was the best!

Then we moved to Arms in 1966. At that time, Arms was just built.

I met all my childhood friends there. We rode bikes, went fishing, and played games at night. I met a great girl and friend, Tindessa. We played hide and go get it and pop the whip. We watched a lot of TV. We loved to watch roller derby, wrestling, and hobble. We also raced cars. We had a lot of friends who had their own race car track, and I had a race car track too. We would go over to each other's house and raced our cars. It was a group of us. We raced Fiver 8 and went Camay racing and drag racing. We raced to see whose cars were the fastest. I won some races and lost some races. My cars were a little red wagon, a Mustang Fastback Cobra, and the 1967 Camaro. I had other cars too. I remember losing in the drag race, but I won in it too! At that time, during the championship drag race, my Mustang Cobra raced against a guy named Preston. He had a little red wagon, and it came down to me and him. Our friends were around to see who would win the championship. Our cars were at the staging area. The lights came on, and our cars were off, and my Mustang Fastback Cobra beat the little red wagon. I was the champion in 1967! It was fun. At that time, we went to the recreation center. We played pool, Ping-Pong, checker, and basketball. We went swimming at Jerry Park's Swimming Pool, and we also had hobbies to race electric cars. My mom loved music. She danced. She went to work. Mom did not get an assistant. We rode in black-and-white cabs.

I grew up with Race Relationships in the Sixties, Taxation without Representation, the March on Washington 1963, the National Association for the Advancement of Colored People, the Civil Rights Bill of 1964, the Voting Act of 1965, human rights, the Kennedys (JFK and Robert), Vietnam, the Apollo program, Martin Luther King Jr., the Poor People's March on Washington in May 1968, Malcolm X, the Ku Klux Klan, President Richard M. Nixon, Motown, rock and roll, Woodstock, and Kent State!

That time for me was the best time of my young life! To experience that whole decade of the sixties! America was going through a great change, and the people were "demanding" that the politicians honor the Constitution of America! ("I pledge allegiance to the Flag of the United States of America and to the Republic for which it stands, one Nation under God, indivisible, with liberty and justice for all!")

When I graduated from Bay Elementary School, I went to Moore Junior High School. When going to Moore, we always stop at Ruby's Food Shop to listen to Motown music before going to school. We were poor. I never met my father. All my life my brothers were in and out of jail. My mother always went to see them in jail. Each month, every other weekend, she took me with her. I remember always sitting in the backseat of the car. Mom took them good food to eat, pop, money, and love. As I grew up, my mother always looked at me as if she didn't like me. At the time I was about nine or ten years old. I was a little boy. I had no role model in my family for me to look up to because my brothers were always in jail. I had great friends in the Arms. We went to other neighborhoods where people had money, and we stole their bikes, not any bikes but wins bike and puffy bikes. A guy named Boy was the first one who brought to the Arms a wins five-speed bike in 1967. It was a new bike. Everyone wanted one! The police were always in Arms looking for stolen bikes. We always hid them till the police left.

I remember when I stole my first bike, it was with a guy named Rob from the Arms. We walked to a place called Kent Park where other people lived, and that's where I stole my first bike. Rob stole a bike too. We walked through the neighborhood because at that time, black people couldn't walk through certain neighborhoods, but back then, black people were fighting for their right, and we didn't care. We saw some bike park in the yard. We looked at them and said, "Let's steal them," and we did. I stole one, and Rob stole one. No one was outside to see us steal them. We got on the bikes and rode off. Back then, we were just kids. It was fun. Kent Park was in the north part of the city. We were riding back to the Arms. When we saw the police, they looked at us, and then they turned their sirens on and pulled us over and asked us where we got the bikes. Of course we lied. We said that our friends said we could ride them. The police officer said the bikes were reported stolen. He put us in the police car and took us to jail. That was the first time I was in jail! I wasn't charged with a crime and was released to my mother.

But as kids, we went back out to steal some more bikes in the other people's neighborhood. This time we got away with the bikes. I stole a wins five-speed stick shift bike where the stick was on the bike and you swift it to get in a gear. It was the newest bike at the time in 1967. My friend also stole a bike that day! We brought them home and rode them. It was the thing back then, just kids growing up! It was a gang of us kids riding together. We went fishing on them and rode down to the river. We went to a place called Devil Drip in the valley and down dirt hills. It was fun. Then late in the summer of 1967, a boy name Danny stole another bike. It was called a Cherry Crate. It was the newest bike back then. Everyone wanted one!

CHAPTER 2

Back then, the adults wore processed in their hair, due rags sunglasses, knit shirt, work pants, silk T-shirts, Taylor shoes, and Long Stars Watches. In 1967, we always played on Able Street. That's where I learned how to play pool at the Second-Century Poolroom. We weren't supposed to be in there as we were just kids, but back then, Red let us play in the back of the poolroom. Red was the owner of the poolroom. Of course there was racism going on throughout my childhood. Racism was all over the country. I was ten years old going on eleven. My brothers were still in jail. I had a sister. Her name was Judy. I liked her. We were good friends. As sister and brother, we did a lot of things together because it was just me and her at home. We took a bath together, played together, watched movies together, went to school together, and went to see our brothers in jail.

During holidays, we did the regular things families do. We always had a turkey and trimmings on Thanksgiving, and Christmas was regular too. My mother got gifts for me and my sister because my other brothers were in jail, so I had a somewhat regular childhood.

In the '60s, it was a trying time in America for blacks and whites, but black people were doing great in spite of all the racial issues and tension. The music set the world on fire. Black people music was changing the state of black people. Motown, the Jackson Five, Stevie Wonder, Martha and the Vandellas, and all the black artists at the time. People love Motown and are still listening to the music today! It will never die! I had a lot to look up to back then, because I didn't have no one to look up to in my family! I was one who was shy and stayed to myself. My friends had fathers. I didn't have a father, just my mother, so growing up, it was just me and my sister. That's when I began to see that my mother's attitude toward me changed. My mother never hugged me. She never told me she loved me. It seemed that I was always alone, no brothers, no father, just me and my sister and my mother, so my friends and their families were my family.

On Friday nights, we watched thriller and scary movies and ate pizza at a friend's house. Back in 1967 and 1968, Classic Clay and Joe Frazier were the big fighters. Kenny Norton too. I was in school at that time at Bay Elementary. I was in the fifth grade and passed the sixth grade, but it seemed that I was always alone with no brothers, no father, to show me guidance to help me grow up, to give me advice, like don't get a job, get a career, go to the military, get a trade plumber or electrician, etc. I had no role model in my family, so I grew up learning things on my own. I also had no mother support. Mom worked a lot back then.

I remember when Martin Luther King Jr. was assassinated on April 4, 1968, and Robert Kennedy on June 5, 1968.

I had a girlfriend. Her name was Cindy. She liked me a lot. I got my first kiss from her. We hung out together. I played football. I was in the Cub Scout. Two years passed. In 1970, I went from sixth grade to seventh grade. I was going to Moore Junior High School. I went to Moore for one year. Mom moved from the Arms to a house in the north of the City on Moon Street. That's when I started going to Hays Junior High School. In that year, I began smoking cannabis. My big brother Joe brought some cannabis home, and my other brother Ray and I tried some cannabis. I didn't like it at first, but the more I tried it, the more I liked it. Growing up, my mom stayed on Moon Street for two years, then she moved to another house up in the north end, a street called Cole Street. It was a nice house. Mom bought it. She always worked hard. From Wayne Street to the Arms to Moon Street to Cole Street, now mom was buying her house. In her mind, she always wanted a house for herself and her kids to live in. That was in 1972. I went to Smith Junior High School. That was the first time I rode a school bus. Back then, a lot of things were going on, such as desegregation and integration. The federal government passed laws to integrate the school system so all Americans can have the right to go to school to get a good education! Smith Junior High was a great school for blacks and white kids. I had lots of friends from my neighborhood who went there, and I met a lot of new friends there! I met my first Caucasian girlfriend there. Her name was Pam. She was fun. We did a lot of things together. Pam and I were always together. When I went home from school, I watched the *Edge of Day* soap operators, then I would go to work on the ice cream truck with Pete for three hours a day, sometimes more. My brothers were always in jail, so I didn't grow up with my brothers. My mother was the one who took care of me. Mom was okay up to then, then she started to change again! I was thirteen going on fourteen years old.

Since I was a little boy, my brothers were always in jail. I found myself in the backseat of a car going to a jail where one of my brothers was. My mother visited Joe and Ray two times a month to bring them money and food and love. She loved and hugged them and supported them, but she showed me no love. That hurt me a lot. My brother Ray got out of jail and came home to love from our mother.

She showed a lot of love for them. My home life wasn't the best, so I went to school and worked on the ice cream truck. My friends helped me a lot.

CHAPTER 3

One day I went to school. It was just another day at school. I liked going to school and doing my schoolwork and was having fun with my friends and my girlfriend Pam. On that day, we were having a math test. We students in the class knew we were going to have a math test that day, so we studied all week for the test. It was my eighth period class, the last class of the day, and we took the test! After the math test, we went where the school bus was waiting to take us home for the day. I got on the school bus, so did my classmates. I was going home to watch the *Edge of Day* and then go help Pete on the ice cream truck. The school bus pulled up to my stop. I got off the school bus, so did some of my friends. We saw a police car setting at the bus stop.

As I walked toward my mother's house, the police officer asked me if I could come over where he was. The police officer said that the person who was with him said that he saw me snatch a lady's pocketbook. I told the police officer that I had been at school all day, and I did not snatch a lady's pocketbook. I said, "I have an eyewitness." I told the police officer that he could come to my mother's house and call the school to see if I was at school all day, so we did. The police officer talked to the principal, and then he got off the phone and said the principal told him that I was in school all day. The police officer said since they had an eyewitness, he had to take me to jail. My mother was standing there, and she said nothing to the police officer. I said I was at school all day, and I didn't snatch a lady's pocketbook.

The police officer put me in handcuffs and called the paddy wagon. They came and put me in the paddy wagon and drove off. They said, "We are taking you to jail!" They threatened me, asking, "Who was your conference?" I said I didn't have a conference. I didn't do anything. Then the police officer in the back of the paddy wagon pulled out a water hole and threatened me, saying he was going to beat me if didn't tell him who was with me when we snatched a lady's pocketbook. I said I didn't snatch a lady's pocketbook, so they took me to jail.

I went to court, and the judge asked, "How do you plead, guilty or not guilty?" I pled not guilty, and then the guard took me back to jail. I was there for about eight weeks. My mother never came to see me when I was in jail. Then my brother came to jail. I didn't know that my brother was up there. One of the youth leaders came and told me that my brother had just come to jail, and my mother was coming to visit him. He told me, "Your mother just wanted to visit him and not you." The guard said she couldn't visit him alone because she had two sons there and couldn't visit one son without the other son. She agreed to see both of us. My mother was very happy to see my brother Ray. My mother didn't say anything to me. She showed me no love but gave my brother everything he needed, so I was there for about ten minutes. Then after the visit, I asked my brother, "What was you doing up here?" He said that he and his friend Rex snatched a lady's pocketbook. I got mad! My brother wouldn't tell the court that I had nothing to do with snatching a lady's pocketbook. But my brother did! He said he wasn't going to snitch on his friend Rex, so my brother lied to the court and said that I was with him! My mother knew that I was at school but didn't say anything to help me! I told the court of point lawyer that I was in school at the time the pocketbook was snatched. My brother and my mother were in the room when I said that to the lawyer. The lawyer said, "Well, they have an eyewitness and said he saw you snatch the lady's pocketbook!"

"No! I was in school!" I replied.

About two and half weeks passed, and I had been in for about ten weeks. My mother came to visit my brother two more times but didn't come to see me. I went to the visiting room, but my mother never talked to me or asked how I was doing.

We finally went to court. I saw my teacher and the principal and the bus driver in the courtroom. I saw my teacher testify. He said, "Brett was in my classroom at the time the pocketbook was snatched. Brett couldn't know about that. He didn't snatch the lady's pocketbook." My teacher further told the court, "Brett was in my classroom the whole time." Then he got off the stand, and my principal got on the stand under oath and testified, "Brett was in school all week and was in school at the time of the crime, so he couldn't have been there to snatch the lady's pocketbook."

All of the testimonies were in, so I went back upstairs to jail. After about twelve weeks I had been in jail, my mother came to visit my brother again on the next visiting day. I had to go because she had two sons in jail. She was so happy to see her son Ray.

The day came to go back to the court to see what the court had decided in front all the people in the courtroom, and the lady whose pocketbook was snatched and my teacher and my principal and my mother and the lawyer and the judge looked at the verdict and looked at me and my brother and asked us to stand up. The court read the verdict. He said, "Brett, the court found you guilty as charged and sentenced you primitively to the Youth Service." After that, the sheriff handcuffed me then chained my feet together and treated me like I killed someone! Then they took me to the country jail for adults. They sentenced my brother to the same thing. My mother hugged him and kissed him, not me. They also took him to the country jail.

That was the first time I was behind bars in an eight-by-eleven cell. There was no room to move. That's where I learned how to masturbate looking at magazines. I stayed in the country jail for two weeks. My mother never came to see me; neither did she write to me. Not sure if she came to see my brother. I think she did! My grandmother came to visit us.

shower once a week read books to pass the time away.

CHAPTER 4

From the country jail, I went to the Juvenile Detention Center. When I got there, it was like I was free! There were no bars. We had cottages to live in. Every morning we had breakfast of half gallon of milk, cereal, and fruit. It was great compared with the country jail. Lunch was the same as breakfast and dinner.

During the day, the youth leader of each cottage would let us go outside and play basketball or whatever. I stayed at the Juvenile Detention Center for about two months. My mother never came to visit me! From the time I went to jail, March 1, 1973, my mother never came to see me! After about five two six months in the institution, I received no letters, no money, nothing, from my mother.

Then they sent me to the Industrial School in the Hills. When I got there, I went to intake to be assigned to a cottage. I was assigned to the Green Cottage. The Green Cottage was assigned to the mess hall or the kitchen to perpetrate food for the inmates' breakfast, lunch, and dinner. That's how I got money for commentary.

Every morning we had to make up our bed tight, and our shoes had to have a shine on them at all times! We took a shower at five o'clock in the morning. After shower, we went to the mess hall to cook breakfast at 6:00 a.m. After breakfast, we cleaned up and went back to the Green Cottage to play cards or went outside to play basketball. Then at lunch, we were back to the mess hall to get lunch ready. After lunch, we went back to the Green Cottage and watched TV, read books, played cards, etc. When it was time for dinner, we went back to the mess hall to prepare. That was my day every day till I got out.

Visiting days were Saturday and Sunday. Every other weekend, parents came to see their sons. They never called my name on visiting days! Seven to eight months had passed, and I had not heard from my mother. The guys in jail asked me if I had a family. I said I had a family, but they didn't like to come to the jail to see me.

There was a lady—her name was Faith—who wrote me letters and sent me money. She was my friend's sister. Faith got me through that time. Faith supported me. I had been in jail for about eight to nine months and was wondering when I was getting out. It had been a long time in jail. I wanted to go home, but there was no love at home for me. In October 1973, I went on a furlough for a week at home. The institution sent home a letter to my mother, telling her that her son was coming home for a week on furlough.

When I got to the bus station in Maine, there was no one there to welcome me home. The Industrial School gave us five dollars, so I got on the bus and went home, but I didn't go home. I went to Faith's home, where there was love for me. I stayed at Faith till late in the evening, then I went to go home. I stayed there for a week. I made the best of it. I met my friends who saw me get off the school bus with them about eight and half months ago.

They asked me how I was doing. I said fine. They were glad to see me, and I was glad to see them. During the time I was at home, I knew that my mother never came to see me. It was hard living there with her. It was sad that my mom felt this way. She never hugged me or said that she loved me. When I remember the time I first went to jail, my mother never supported me.

The time to go back to the institution had come. My mother never said goodbye to me. She never hugged me, and she never said that she loved me! I'm sure she went to see my brother Ray in jail. My mother had another son, my eldest brother, Joe. He and Ray were always in the institution when I was growing up. My mother always went to see them on visiting day. I remember that because I was always in the backseat of the car going to see my brothers in jail. My mother was so happy to see them. I was just a little boy then, but I remember.

When they got out of the institution, my mother always went to get them at the bus station, or someone always took her to get them.

So you see how I felt when I went to the institution for nothing. My mother never came to visit me!

I got on the bus and went back to the institution by myself! When I got back to the Industrial School—that was at the end of October—I talked to the social worker and asked him when I would be getting out of there. He said November 27, 1973, so the remaining time I had left there, I did what I did when I got there: worked at the mess hall, read books, played cards, etc.

Maybe a week before I was to come home on that next visiting day, my name was called. All of the inmates knew that my name was never called. Everyone looked at me and said, "You got a visit." So after about nine months went by, I finally got a visit from my mother, my sisters Judy Wanda and Sue, and my baby brother Ben. When I went upstairs, I didn't know what to say to my mother. She never sent me a card. She never sent me money, no love, nothing. I was going up in the visiting room, and I saw them sitting there. I sat down, and I can't remember what we talked about.

The visit was over, so I went back downstairs.

The day came when it was time for me to go home. Everyone in the Green Collage wished me well. I like the guys I met at the institution. They were all right with me! They were from all over the state of Maine.

The guards came and got me, and we went to another cottage where other inmates were also waiting to go home.

When the bus was loaded, we waved and left the institution. I was finally free! I was going home.

When I got to the bus station, there was no one waiting for me. If it wasn't for the Industrial School that gave us five dollars, I wouldn't have a way home. So I went to the bus stop and got on the bus going home, but when I got to my bus stop to get off, I didn't go home. I went to Faith's house. She sent me money and love. I stayed there for hours, then I went home. When I got there, the door was locked. I knocked. No one came to the door. I knocked some more. Finally my mother opened the door. She wasn't glad to see me when I looked at her, so I went to my bedroom to sleep.

When I was rested, I went to the houses of my friends who were on the school bus when we all got off that day. They were glad to see me. They asked me how I was doing. I said, "Great! It is nice to be back home."

I had to see a parole officer. I didn't want to talk to him because I didn't do anything. I had a bad attitude, but I saw him. After that, I went back to my friends' homes.

After that, I had to go to Hayes Base to go to school, so I went there. It was an adult day school. I was a juvenile. Why I was there, I do not know.

I got out of Hayes Base and went back to a regular school. I went back to the school I was going to before I went to jail, Smith Junior High School. The teacher who testified was glad to see me. He knew that I went to jail for nothing! I also saw the principal who testified in court for me. They knew I went to jail for nothing! But anyway, I graduated from Smith Junior High School.

CHAPTER 5

Now I was in the tenth grade in high school. I went to Carlo High School for a year and then transferred to Raymond High School and stayed there for two years. When I graduated, my mother didn't come to my Graduation, so I didn't go. But I remember when my sister was to graduate, my mother was so glad to go to her graduation. That hurt me!

So I was out of school. I was nineteen years old. I was out of school for a week, and my mother wanted me out of her house! I told her that I had nowhere to go! She said, "You are grown now, Brett. I took care of you for eighteen years of your life. Now you have to go take care of yourself!" I told her I had nowhere go! She called the police on me and had them take me out of her house. The police said if I had no pace to go, they would take me to jail for vacancy! I left and went to Faith's house and stayed there.

I stayed there for a while, but because her boyfriend didn't want me to stay there, which I understood, I left and went to my friend's house and asked his mother, Mrs. Betty, if I could stay there for a while. She had three girls there, and I know all of them. Mrs. Betty said yes, I could stay there as long as I needed to, and I said, "Thank you, Mrs. Betty."

It was different there, but I got used to it. I felt that my mother never liked me as her son. She never told me who my father was. She said he was dead. I asked her where he was buried. She said she didn't know.

I stayed at Mrs. Betty for about two months. I started to drive a cab and started to make some money. I gave Mrs. Betty some money for letting me stay there, and then I got my first apartment out in Chester. My address was 65 Chester Ct.

It was great that I didn't have to live with my mother anymore. The only things I had were my TV, my stereo, and my car. As I worked driving a cab, I was thinking about my life. I just got out of jail. My mother never came to see me, except the week before I was to come home. She never showed me love like her other kids. I was the only one she kicked out of her house, so I was out here on my own!

I worked hard to get the things I wanted! I got a sofa, a chair, a table, and a telephone for my apartment.

I met a girl in my apartment building. Her name was Kate. She was a nice girl. We became friends, then later we became lovers!

I lived in Chester for about two years, then I met a girl. Her name was Anita. We began to talk, and then we became friends and then lovers. I moved in with her in 1982. We had a great time together. Anita was in a relationship when I met her, but she didn't like her boyfriend because he was cheating on her, so she left him for me. Anita had kids: a daughter named Trisha and two sons named Jay and Richard. They liked me, and I liked them. Anita was from Portland, Maine. We went back and forth to Portland to see her mom, but her mom didn't like me. Why? I didn't know. Her mom and her mom's sister would come down to see Anita and the kids. I would cook for them.

That went on for years. I wanted to marry Anita, but she didn't want anything out of life. She just wanted to stay on assistance. I wanted more out of life! I knew I was going to leave her. I went to work one night. I delivered pizzas for Pizza Talk. I was going on my last run for the night. I went out to my car, and I saw a lady standing at the bus stop. She asked me if I knew what time the bus got there. I said I didn't know. I asked her where she was going. She said, "I'm going to an employer's meeting."

I said, "If you like, I can take you to your meeting, after I dropped off this pizza." She said okay, so I helped her into my car, and I dropped off the pizza, went back to the station, and clocked out.

I took Rhonda to her meeting and waited on her. We began to talk. I took her back to the bus stop where I met her. She said, "Thank you, Brett." Then she asked, "Do you have a phone number?"

I said, "Yes, do you want it?" She said yes, so I gave her my number, and I left and went home, where I was living with Anita.

Rhonda called me the next day. We began to talk. She told me that she was married and was in an abusive relationship. She said she wanted a divorce but was scared of her husband, so I supported her. Rhonda said that she had a lawyer and that he was helping her to get a divorce.

Rhonda said that she was from South Carolina, but her family moved to Maryland, and her husband was from Vermont.

I told Rhonda that I was living with a lady. I told her that I wanted to marry her, but Anita didn't want anything out of life but to be on assistance! I had told Anita before I met Rhonda that I was going to leave her. I didn't want to live with Anita anymore. I wanted something out of life! There were some police officers coming out to where Anita was living to intimidate black guys, but I wasn't intimidated by the police officers. They were trying to get me. For what, I don't know. One day I ordered a sub from Mr. B's Pizza. I went out to my car to go get my sub. I saw the police out there, but I went to go get my sub. They followed me when I was on the city street. They turned on their sirens. I kept going to get my sub. I got to Mr. B's Pizza to get my sub, and they came in, and one of the officers put his hand on me. I pulled away from him. He put his hand on me again, and I grabbed him. We fell down on the floor, and the other officers grabbed me and pulled me off the other officer. By that time, there were about ten officers there. The captain asked me what happened. I told him that I was going to pick up my order from Mr. B's Pizza. I told the captain that the officer out where I live at was trying to intimidate the black guys out there, including me, but I wasn't scared of them, so when I went out to my car to go get my sub, they followed me. When I got on the city street, they turned on their sirens. I kept going to Mr. B's Pizza. I didn't do anything.

I got out of my car and went inside to pick up my sub. They came in. One officer put his hand on me. I pulled away, and he put his hand on me again and said, "Come with me." I said, "What did I do?" He said, "Come with me." I pulled away again. He grabbed me again, and I grabbed him, and we fell to the floor. The other officers grabbed me and got me off the officer. I told the captain that they never told me what I did. It was all a lie. The captain said, "We will have to take you downtown for screening."

I told the judge the same thing. They gave me two weekends in the workhouse. After that, my attitude changed, and I wasn't scared or intimidated by law enforcement! I went to jail for nothing again! That's twice! Now this has changed me forever.

CHAPTER 6

I **did the two weekends in** the workhouse. My life has changed, so I began to date Rhonda. She was going through a lot. I supported her. After about two months, we were out one night, and Rhonda said to me that she wanted me to meet her kids the next day. I said okay. I dropped her off that night, and the next day, I went to where she lived. When I pulled up, I saw her with all of her kids. I was surprised, but I was glad to see her and her kids. I liked her kids. I didn't have kids of my own, so we all got into my car and went to the park. We had lunch and ice cream. I got to know the kids' names, her daughters Mailko Ayana, her sons Landon Logan twins, and Jayden and they knew my name.

Rhonda seemed happy. She had been under a lot of pressure, so it was good to see her at peace. That next week, Rhonda told me that she had a lawyer, and he was going to help her get a divorce. I said great, and I supported her. That went on for months. One day, I was coming home from work when I saw a hearse and some funeral cars with my whole family in them. It caught me by surprise! I didn't know that my mother's sister had passed away. No one called or told me, so I turned around and followed the hearse and the funeral cars. They went to a church where the funeral was held. I saw my family get out of the funeral cars. They didn't see me because I was far back in the funeral line. I felt bad because I wasn't invited, so I finally parked and went into the church. Then I saw my grandmother. When I looked at my grandmother, she cried. It seemed like she knew that her daughter, my mother, didn't call me. Why, I didn't know, but it was always like that when it came to my family. For some reason, my mother never liked me but loved her other children. I was hurt. After the funeral and my aunt was put back in the hearse and my family got back in the funeral cars, my grandmother said, "Brett, I will ride with you."

I said, "Okay, Grandma." We got in my car, and I asked her why Mom didn't tell me that Aunt Linda passed away. Grandma just looked at me and shook her head and said she didn't know.

When we got to the burial site, that's when my family saw me. They really didn't say anything to me because none of them cared enough to call me to let me know that Aunt Linda had died. I didn't feel like family. After the funeral, my family got into the funeral cars and left, and I took Grandma back home. I went back home to where I was living, at Anita's house. I told Anita what had happened. She knew that my family didn't support me, and that day ended too. The next day, Rhonda finally got her divorce. She was so happy. Rhonda's step grandmother helped her with the kids. She kept the kids for Rhonda while Rhonda was getting herself together.

At that time, Anita had kicked me out of her house, but she let me come back the next day. I talked to Anita and told her that we had been living together for five years, and we hadn't gotten anywhere. I told her that I was going to leave her if she didn't want to do anything. I was trying to get a house or something, but she just wanted to stay on assistance. I told her that I was going to leave her. I wanted to leave her even before I met Rhonda. At this time, Anita knew I was seeing someone. Rhonda sometimes came by Anita's house and threw pebbles at the basement window, because I slept in the basement, to get me out with her. I think Anita saw Rhonda. At that time, I was ready to leave Anita, so a couple of weeks went by, and I left Anita. However, Rhonda and I didn't have anywhere to go. Knowing how my mother called the police on me and kicked me out of her house, knowing that I was in jail for nothing and she never came to see me but one time, a week before I was to come home, knowing all that, I still asked her if I could stay there with my girlfriend, and she said no! While my brothers could stay there, I could not, so Rhonda and I slept in my car every night and went to restaurants to wash up. That went on for about one month. I asked my mother if we can wash up in her house. She didn't want me to, but she said okay, so Rhonda and I slept in my car and washed up in her house. After about one and half months, Rhonda and I got an apartment in Sand Square. It was a nice apartment. I was working at Pizza Talk, and she was studying at the Newton School. Things were going good for Rhonda, so she wanted to get her kids from her stepgrandmother. We went through that. I supported her through all of it.

Rhonda got her kids, and we all lived in the apartment. She sent her kids to school. After everything was settled, Rhonda wanted to go back home to let her family know that things were better for her and her kids, and she wanted them to meet me, so we went to Maryland to visit her family. We got there, and everyone was so happy to see Rhonda and her kids and me. There were tears and hugs and laughter. Her mom made a great dinner for us. I was glad to see Rhonda and her family reunited again. I had never been to Maryland. I liked it over there. I drove to Baltimore, Maryland. It was a big city. I went back to the house of Rhonda's mother, where we had dinner and talked with her family. We talked about getting married and buying a home and how the kids were doing good in school.

We left Maryland and returned home to Maine. We started to plan for our wedding.

Rhonda and I were going to take back some movies that we had rented from buster movies. As we were going down the street, a car came out in front of us and hit my car. The crash was so hard that it broke Rhonda's leg. We were getting married in a couple of weeks. They took Rhonda to the hospital and put her leg in a cast. The doctor told Rhonda she can still get married, and he would take the cast off for that day, so Rhonda told her family that the wedding was still on! It was hard for me to ask my family to come because of all I went through with my family, but they came.

Rhonda and I got married. We were both so happy. I was happy because I had never been married before. After the wedding, my wife and I went to Ms. Goodwin's house. She was the grandmother of my best friend Jack, and she was like a mother and a grandmother to me. She cared when no one cared! Ms. Goodwin was glad to see us. Rhonda was in her wedding dress, and I was in my tuxedo. We couldn't do much because Rhonda's leg was still broken. We left Ms. Goodwin's home and went to our apartment. It was a great experience for us. We were now man and wife!

CHAPTER 7

I talked to my friend Reed about trying to buy a house. His mother was in real estate, so we got together with my friend's mother, Mrs. Park, and talked to her about buying a house. She helped us look at some houses, but they weren't what we were looking for, so Mrs. Park showed us a house on Pine Street. It was the house we were looking for. It had three bedrooms, it had a basement, and it had a two-car garage and a carport. Rhonda and I liked it and told Mrs. Park that we would like to buy the house, so she got the paperwork ready for us. The next day, I opened the store. At that time, I was working at Pizza Talk as a dough master and a shift manager. I liked working at Pizza Talk. When I opened the store, I noticed that it was not cleaned the previous night, and the paperwork wasn't done. I knew the manager, Doug, was coming in to open the store. When Doug came in, he saw the store was not clean and the nightly paperwork wasn't done. He was mad! I was doing my job. Collin was the manager on duty that night. Doug called Collin, but Collin never called Doug back. We got behind that day. I prepped the dough for the day and helped Doug in cleaning the store, so Doug called in another manager, Steve. Doug was so mad that day that he left the store. Steve and I ran lunch, and I prepped veggies for dinner, and my shift was over. The next day, I went in to open the store. There was a note on the table saying that Collin never called in. Collin was to open the store that day, so Doug said, "If Collin comes in, have him call me!" When Collin came in that morning, I told him, "Doug wants you to call him." Collin was mad about something. He said, "I am not going to call Doug. Forget this job!" Collin called me a nigger and left the store. I was shocked that Collin called me a nigger!

When I first met Collin, he was a great coworker. I liked him a lot! He helped me a lot! Collin had just gotten a new car, and he was putting in a new stereo and asked me if I would like his old stereo. I said yes. Collin said, "Okay, Brett, it is yours."

I replied, "Thanks, Collin." It was a nice stereo. It was a Pioneer. Collin said, "Brett, when I put my new stereo in my car, I will put my old stereo in your car."

I said, "Cool." That was the kind of person Collin was. He invited me and my wife to his parties. My wife had just bought a new car, and I drove it up to work. Collin was the opening manager that day. I always opened the store to prep dough and veggies.

Collin pulled up and came in the store and asked, "Whose new car is that outside?"

I replied, "It's my wife's car."

He said, "Nice. I like it." Collin and I went outside to look at it. He said it was nice, so he sat in it, turned on the stereo, and said, "Factory radio sucks." Collin said, "Brett, I know where your wife can get a better stereo for her car. I could get it at a discounted price." I knew the stereo in her car was factory, so I said, "Get it, Collin."

He said, "Okay, Brett, I will, and when I get it, I will put it in for her."

"That's great!"

Collin did get the stereo, and he did put it in for us. That's the kind of person Collin was!

Doug had other assistant managers and shift managers. They were all okay coworkers.

One manager, Tony, was all right with me. He also helped me. I met his wife and kids and had been to his home.

One time, Tony was telling me that he didn't like the way the store was operating. The other managers weren't doing their jobs, paperwork wasn't getting done, and employees weren't showing up for their shifts, so Tony said he was going over to Little Castles because the opportunities there were great. He will be the store manager. He told me, "Brett, when I get my store operating, I will call you to come over because I can get you a store!"

I replied, "Thanks, Tony."

I called Doug and told him that Collin was not going to call him. Doug was so mad. It was his day off, but he had to come in to close the store. When Doug got in the store, he started to tell me what to do. I knew what to do! At that time, Doug didn't care about anything. He took it out on me! I told him, "I will help you, but you do not have to talk to me like this, Doug."

He said, "Do what I told you to do!"

I replied, "Okay, after I finish prepping my dough for the day."

"I want you to do what I told you to do now!"

I said, "Doug, you know the dough has to be prepped."

He then said, "You're fired!"

"You can't fire me. I didn't do anything."

Doug said, "Brett, you didn't do what I told you to do."

"Doug, you didn't respect my position. As you know, it takes time for the dough to proof! I know you are mad because Collin didn't come in, but, Doug, it's not right that you take it out on me!"

"Brett, you have to leave the store." Doug fired me the day before my wife and I were too close on our new home! We were already approved for the loan. We just had to sign some paperwork and to pay the closing cost, and the deal was done. Just before my wife and I were to sign the papers, I asked Mrs. Park if I could talk to her. She and I went outside, and I told her what just happened to me on my job. I was fired. She said, "The deal is already done. You just have to go inside and sign some papers." We went back inside, and my wife and I signed some papers, and the deal was done. My wife and I just bought our new home. We moved in our new home, and we, including the kids, were very happy. We bought the house in May 1992. We moved in it in July 1992.

When we settled in our new home, my wife began to enroll the kids in a nearby school. She enrolled them at East Park Elementary School.

CHAPTER 8

The old assistant manager of Pizza Talk knew that Doug knew that I was coming over to Little Castles. Tony knew that Doug had just fired me. He called me two days after I was fired and said, "I hear that Doug fired you, Brett. I have an assistant manager position for you. When can you start?"

I said, "Tomorrow."

Tony said, "Come tomorrow at 10:00 a.m., and I will have your uniforms ready for you and introduce you to your new crew, and I can get you your own store in time." I was grateful. "Thank you, Tony. Yes, I would like to work with you, Tony, and to learn how to run Little Castles." I started to work at Little Castles and learn the operations: opening and closing, paperwork, inventory, food temperature, payroll, hiring, firing, interviewing, etc. I got really good at running the store. My wife was so happy that I got the job with my old manager. My wife worked at Beach Park.

Halloween came, and we took the kids to their school Halloween party. The kids loved it, and my wife and I loved it too! Rhonda was finally happy after all she had gone through. I was happy for her. She saw that the kids were happy. We took pictures and ate food. It was a great time for all of us.

Work was going good for me and my wife! Rhonda cooked our first Thanksgiving dinner in our new house. I could see Rhonda was so happy. I was the stepdad, but I was a father to her kids.

Then Christmas came, and we had a great first Christmas. My wife decorated the house and put up a Christmas tree. She cooked a great Christmas dinner. I watched football while the kids played with their toys. It was a great time for the Jones family. We had been spending the holidays in our house, and then we would experience New Year together as well.

Going into New Year 1993, things were going good for me and my wife. Her family was very happy that her new husband was doing a great job with the kids and the new home. There was work for me, and my wife was doing good! I loved my store, and Rhonda loved her job. The kids loved their new school, so we were just one big happy family.

The winter of 1993 was bad, but we made it through. Spring came, and Rhonda and I were making plans to go to South Carolina for her grandfather and grandmother's twenty-fifth wedding anniversary.

The time came for me and my family to go to South Carolina. I had never been to South Carolina, so it was a great time for me. We packed up the car and went to South Carolina. The kids were very happy. It was a long ride going down South. We went through lots of states. I liked going through West Virginia and Virginia, and we went through North Carolina—that's where I saw red dirt for the first time in my life! My wife said that they used to eat it. I said, "What, y'all ate it?"

She said, "Everyone down South eats red dirt."

We were going to a place called Hill, South Carolina. We finally got to her grandfather and grandmother's house. It was a long ride, but we loved it! Rhonda's family from Maryland hadn't gotten there yet. Rhonda's grandmother and grandfather were so happy to see their granddaughter and her kids and her new husband. They had a lot of food. You always hear people from down South love grits and eggs, and they did. We all ate breakfast. I was tired, so I sat on the sofa and napped for a while. Rhonda's family finally made it to Grandma and Granddad's house. Rhonda's mother was so happy to see her daughter and her grandkids and me. That day came to an end, and a new day began. It was time to go to the twenty-fifth wedding anniversary celebration of her grandmother and grandfather. We followed her family to the church, where the event was to be held. When we pulled up to the church, it had a graveyard in front of it. I had never seen that before. Everything was so green. The trees were straight up, and the grass was very green. We were in the woods somewhere in South Carolina. It was a great celebration! We packed up and went back to Granddad and Grandma's house and ate dinner with her family and friends. After dinner, everyone wanted to get to know me! So we talked. I told them about me, and they were so happy that I helped Rhonda and the kids get away from her ex-husband. They all liked me. That made me feel good! The next day, we spent time looking around Hill. They had lots of old shacks there. They looked like Old Slave Home, where slaves used to live by the cotton fields. It was very hot down there. I talked to some old people, and they told me lots of things that happened down there in Hill, how they worked in plantations, how their parents were slaves. I took pictures of the old houses. It was getting late in the evening. We went back to her grandma and granddad's home.

Rhonda talked to her family, and the kids played with their relatives. I just watched everyone. Rhonda was talking to her cousin, and her cousin was telling Rhonda everyone was getting a divorce. I heard that. Later that evening, I was talking to my wife and told her that I heard them talking about everyone was getting a divorce in their family. I asked Rhonda if she was going to divorce me. She said no. The next day, it was time for us to go back home to Maine. Her grandma and granddad and her family fixed us a great breakfast and packed us some sandwich to take with us on the way back to Maine. When it came time for us to leave, there were lots of hugs, tears, and smiles. They hugged me, and I hugged them. The grandparents hugged the kids and hugged their granddaughter Rhonda. We got into the car, and back to Maine we went.

CHAPTER 9

We got back to Maine. It was the summer of 1993. It was great. We took the kids swimming. We went to the Bangor State Fair and had a great time. We took pictures and enjoyed the rides. The kids loved it, and my wife, Rhonda, was so happy for the first time in a long time. I could see Rhonda was free of everything she went through before she met me. I was happy for her.

My wife bought a car, and she never told me about it. She began to be very secretive. She went on assistance and didn't tell me! While I was working hard to keep the Jones family going, my wife was planning to leave me, but I didn't know! She started to get bold with me. I didn't know what was going on. She started doing things on her own, taking the kids places without me. She kept getting phone calls. I trusted my wife, so I didn't think anything of it, but I knew something was up. I couldn't put my finger on it.

A new school year came. The kids were happy because all of them graduated to the next grade. The day before the first day of school, Rhonda did the girls' hair and I cut the boys' hair. They were all ready to go to school. When the next day came, I got up as usual. Rhonda was up, and the kids were also up. I got ready for work. I told the kids to have a great day at school. I kissed them and kissed my wife, and off to work I went. I had a great day at work. My wife didn't call me. She always called me. I didn't think anything of it. I went home after working all day, came into the house, and put my keys on the table, where I saw a letter. I picked it up and began to read it. My life just changed. My wife had left me. She said in the letter that she was leaving me not because I did something wrong, but she wanted to go back home and live with her family. I called my sisters to see if they knew where Rhonda was. They said no. I went to the school where the kids were going and asked the secretary if my stepkids were inside. She said that their mom came and got them out of school early that day. I got scared! I was a mess. All day after work, I looked for my wife! Then I called her mother's house, and Rhonda was there. I asked her why she left me. She said, "I wanted to tell you, but I thought that you wouldn't like it, so I wrote a letter and left it for you to read when you came home."

"Rhonda, you have done this to me after everything I did for you. You wasn't a lady enough to tell me what you was up to!"

She didn't say anything, so now things began to make sense because of the way she was acting. Rhonda said, "Brett, I'm coming back. I just need some time for me and the kids." I was hurt that she did that to me! I went to work, and behind my back my wife left me!

It was hard for me. I was in a lot of pain, but I knew that I had to be strong! I had no family support. They knew but didn't support me! I was on my own! It was hard for me. All of a sudden, the mortgage and all the bills were on me! I didn't know how I was going to do it! I lost weight, but I went to work every day. My manager, Tony, knew that my wife had left me. He was a great help to me. He did everything he could to make things easy for me. Work helped me out a lot because it gave me something to do and kept my mind off what just happened to me. Everyone at work helped me, and my supervisor helped me too. She called my wife and talked to her then asked her, "Why did you leave your husband?" I was sitting there with her. She asked my wife if she still loved me, and the look on her face told me that my wife said no! My supervisor gave me the phone. I knew my wife was lying to make me out to be a bad guy. Only Rhonda and I knew what I did for her and the kids. I needed help from my family, but they weren't there for me. I was all by myself! My mother laughed at me, as if she hoped I would lose my home. The look in her eyes! My mother never came over to give me comfort. She never came over to support me when her son needed her! I was by myself. I was scared and alone, no father, no mother. But my sister Wanda helped me out a lot. She was someone I could talk to. My other sister, Judy, also helped me. My brothers were in jail. They never helped me all my life because they were always in jail.

One day during that time, I came home from work and opened my back door to enter my house and saw a bag. It caught me by surprise. I picked it up and went inside and opened it up. There was a picture frame with my mother in it. I didn't know what to think because she never showed me love. I put it on the mantel in my living room and kept it there for about two days, but I just couldn't keep it there. I took it back and put in her mailbox. Why would a mother do that to her son who was fighting for his life? I needed my mother's support but not like that! My mother must have been keeping a secret from me all my life. I don't know if I was a wanted child. But all indications show that my mother didn't love me!

Each day was hard for me, not knowing what my wife was doing. She wasn't calling like she said she would. I would call her mom's house, but no one would pick up the phone. It was tough for me. It was unbelievable! Time passed. It had been two months since my wife left me, and I know that I had to get another job. I went out to look for a another job. I got a part-time job as a night cleaner four hours a night, Monday through Friday. That was helping me out to make ends meet, so I kept working. I was paying my bills and the mortgage and eating. Things started to get better, but it was still hard for me. The holidays came and went. I was all by myself. The year 1993 came to an end, and 1994 began. I was proud of myself for not giving up! I kept saying to myself that I was going to do this! I wasn't going to let anything get to me because of everything I had to go through when I was growing up. I still was hoping that my wife would come back home, but as time went by, hope started to fade. Maybe God wanted me to go through this. Maybe it was a test. I don't know.

The year 1994 arrived. I worked hard. My mom never gave me any support. She never called to ask me how I was doing. She never came over to bring me food. There was no support! But that's all right because she never helped me anyway. At that time, I needed to be by myself, and this was the hand I was dealt with. I had to play it, so I did! Among everything that I had been through, this was the hardest. I was determined to make it with no family support. I believe in me! In all of the events I had to go through in my life, no one was ever there for me, but I was there for me! So 1994 came to an end, and a new year came, 1995. I was doing all right. I was proud of myself for doing what I needed to do to keep my home and to pay my bills. I was still working two jobs. To show you how God works, I got promoted to a new store of Little Castles in Hampden. I worked there for some time, then a managerial job opened, and my manager, Tony, told me, "Now is the time, Brett, to get your own store!"

Tony took me over to the new store. He knew I knew how to open and close the store and do the paperwork. Tony new I was ready, so he went to the corporation's office and suggested that I be the new manager at the Land Store. The corporation trusted Tony's opinion, so while at work, Tony called and told me that he had good news for me. He didn't say what the good news was. I had no idea what it was. Later that day, Tony came to his store on Rose Road with his wife and kids. He was a great guy! He always believed in me. Tony asked me how my day was going. I said good, and his wife looked at me. They both knew what I was going through then. Tony told me the good news. "The good news is that now you have your own store, Brett." That was the best news I had ever heard. It was great! I was the new manager at the Land Store that was great new for me!

I got my own store, and I was so proud!

The next day, Tony and I went over to the Land Store. No one was there because the old manager was out, and I was the new manager. I knew how to run the store because I did it at Rose, so Tony and I looked around the store. We noticed that the store was very dirty! Tony and I started to clean it. The shift manager who closed that night left a note on the table to let us know who was opening the store that day and what he had done at closing. The shift manager came in to open the store. Tony and I Introduced ourselves to the manager. He began to tell us how the store was doing. He said that the old manager didn't care about the store, that's why sales were down. He didn't keep the store clean. The customers said the food wasn't good! They had employees who had long hair and didn't wear a hairnet. Tony and I left the opening manager alone so he could do his job. He knew what to do to get the store ready for opening, so we left the store because I was closing that night. I went home and did something around the house. I was happy because I just got a look at my store and looked forward to closing that night.

I went in at 2:00 p.m. The opening manager did a great job of getting the store ready for dinner rush. He had dough prepped and had cheese and veggies ready for me. The store was clean. Everything looked good! I knew I had a great shift manager, so he left and told me who was coming in for the night. When the crew started coming in, they knew that it was going to be a new manager in the store that night. I introduced myself to them, and they started to tell me things about the store and how the old manager hired his friend and they got away with everything! That's why the store sales were down. I told them, "That's why I'm here!" I started to look at the paperwork and checked the inventory while the crew started running the store. I was just observing them. The dinner rush started, and the crew were doing a good job. The customers started coming in and saw a new manager and saw that the store was clean and the crew looked great. I showed the crew how to make a sub bun, how to make a great pizza and salads, how to put popes seed and garlic cheese on the crust, and how to weigh the toppings. Some of the old customers started to call in and tell us how good the pizza tasted and that the food tasted better. That was good news! It was a great first night. I closed the store. The opening manager whom I met early in the day was opening the next day, so I felt good about everything at closing, and everything was ready for him. I was to close the next day. I called Tony and told him how the first night went. I told him that I had a great crew and looked forward to training them better to make a great product! Tony said, "Great job, Brett. I know you can get the job done!"

CHAPTER 10

The next day, I went in to close. The day manager did a great job! I began to interview high school kids to work part-time evening to give them a sense of responsibility and job training and to earn some money. I hired four crew members. I trained them, and it went great. The crew members' shift was 4:00 p.m. to 8:00 p.m. on weekdays and, on weekends, if their parents were okay with it, 5:00 p.m. to 11:00 p.m. The store was doing good. Sales were up, and we were getting great comments from our customers. The corporation was happy, so it was a great experience. The high school kids I hired were very happy to work at the Land Store. They came to work when they were scheduled, so months and months passed, and the store was doing great. In December 1995, the area manager came in the store and talked to me and then told me that the store was closing. They stopped the operation that night. I didn't like it because we were right in the middle of dinner rush. It was sad that they did that. As the manager, I felt that they should have told me in advance that they were going to close the store! I could have put a sign in the window to let the customers know that the store was going to be closing in two weeks and let them know where the next store was, but the corporation just came in and closed the store! I couldn't say anything, so they closed the store at Land.

The next day, Tony called me, and he said, "Brett, you will be okay." I had to go to the corporation's office, where they told me that I did a great job at the Land Store, increasing the sales, but the store was too far gone for saving. They promoted me to area supervisor, which means I was given three stores: the Crown, the Beach, and the Bowl Store.

I went home that day. As I was reading my mail, I saw an attorney's letter, so I started to read it. My wife had filed for a divorce. The letter stated, "You can sign these documents and get a divorce and keep the house, or you can contest it and go to trial, and nine times out of ten, you would lose the house, and Rhonda will get half of the property's selling price." I signed the document, and I was divorced.

The next day at about 10:00 a.m., I went around to my stores to check on the managers and see how their store was doing. The first store I went to was Crown to meet the manager of the store. Her name was Kelly. I wanted to talk to her to see if she needed anything. As I looked around her store, it was clean. Food prep looked good. The walk-in was at the right temperature. The perishable food was dated and wrapped. All pizza products were dated. I looked at the paperwork, time sheets, payroll, inventory, plus or minus hours—everything looked good. I had a good manager at the Crown Store, so I stayed at Crown and helped her with the lunch rush. I was coming back to Crown that night to meet the closing manager, Rhonda, and to meet the staff. I came back and met the closing manager. She was great. She ran a good shift, and she was happy to meet me. My next store was Beach. When I got there, the manager was expecting me, so I introduced myself. He told me his name was Tom. I asked him how things were going. He said okay, so I looked around the Beach Store. It was clean. They had just finished lunch. They did a great lunch. The staff were cleaning the store after lunch. I liked that. I checked the paperwork, and it looked good. I looked at time sheets, payroll, plus or minus hours, inventory—all looked good. I went in the walk-in. Perishable foods were dated and wrapped, the walk-in was at the right temperature, so everything looked good. The manager at the store was on his job, so I left, but I told the manager that I would be back that evening to meet the closing manager.

I returned to Beach at 6:00 p.m., and I met the closing manager. She was great! Her name was Michelle. She also ran a good shift. Everyone was at their station. Dinner rush was starting, and I helped them through it. The manager at Beach liked the idea that I stayed to help through dinner, and I said, "That's what we do at Little Castles. We are a team." She said, "I like that." I left for the evening.

The next store I visited was Bowl. When I got there, the manager was waiting on me. I introduced myself to her, and she told me her name was

Tammy. I asked her how things were going. She said great. The staff were wearing clean uniforms. The store was clean. The staff were preparing for dinner rush. I looked around her store and looked at the paperwork, payroll, plus or minus hours, inventory, etc. I walked in the walk-in. Perishable food was dated, pizza sauce was made, cheese was cut up, and the walk-in was at the right temperature. I stayed at Bowl for dinner rush. The crew did a great job running dinner rush.

All three stores I visited were in great shape, and they all had great managers!

CHAPTER 11

A **couple of months went by.** One day Tony called me, asking me how things were going. I said great! Tony was telling me that he was hearing that some stores were closing. He said he didn't know which ones were going to be closing. He said he would let me know. I said okay. About two weeks went by, and Tony called me again and said that they were closing a lot of stores. He said, "Brett, two of your stores, the Crown and the Beach, were going to close." He didn't say when, but they going to close. I said, "Thanks, Tony, for letting me know."

A week went by. The corporation called me and said Crown and Beach were closing, so I went to the stores and told the managers the stores were closing, and I would see about getting the crew members to transfer to other stores. I got all the staff who wanted to transfer and got them into other stores.

The next week, I went to the corporation's office, and they told me that they wanted me to go to the Bowl Store to help out because they were closing a lot of stores. I said okay, and I went to the Bowl to help out. The staff were great! After about a month, some of the staff started to dislike me. I didn't know why, but they did! One day I got a call from Tony saying that a female employee said that I sexually harassed her. I told him I didn't. He said the corporation was going to investigate and that I was to leave the store. I asked why. He said because they were going to investigate the allegation. I was shocked. I said, "Tony, I didn't do anything."

Tony said, "Brett, I know!"

I left the store. About a week went by. Tony called me and said that I was fired! He explained, "Some of the crew said that you were sexually harassing them." I'm black and they were white. I do not know if that was the case, but I was fired. It was unfair. I got a lawyer and told him what

I was accused of. I told the attorney that a female employee said that I sexually harassed her. The attorney asked me if they had any evidence on me. I said no. He asked me if anyone from Little Castles officially told me why I was discharged. I said yes. The attorney asked what my position was. I said, "I worked as a dough master and shift manager, then Little Castles promoted me to manager of a failing store and asked me if I can bring that store back up. I told the corporation that I was excited for the opportunity. I told them that I would bring the store back up, and I did! Sales were better in a week than the store did in a month! Then they closed my store and then made me the area supervisor. I had three stores. They closed two of my stores and made me the manager of the Bowl Store."

The attorney asked me, "You were a manager, and you had your own store, and you were an area supervisor, Brett. You were all that and they still fired you?" I said yes. The attorney said, "Something doesn't sound right." He said that he would take my case. I paid a retainer, and I went looking for employment.

About two weeks went by, and the attorney called me and asked if I could come in to the office. I said yes. The next day I went in. He told me that Little Castles said that I quit. I said no, they fired me. The lawyer looked at me as if I quit. I was readily mad at this time. The attorney asked me if I wanted to continue. I said yes. They fired me because a female employee said I sexually assaulted her. I paid the attorney's fee. It didn't seem like the lawyer was helping me. He didn't give me any hope. I left the attorney's office and went back home.

About a month went by, and I hadn't heard anything from the attorney, so I called him. He said that he hadn't heard anything, so I asked, "So where are we on the Little Castles case?

The attorney replied, "Little Castles said you quit, and you said that they fired you, Brett. Do you have any paperwork stating that you were fired for sexually assaulting a female employee?"

I said, "No, they didn't give me any paper stating that."

The attorney said, "Without that, it's going to be hard to pursue the case that they fired you for sexually assaulting a female employee." I paid the attorney good money, and he just told me that was it going to be hard to pursue the case! I was disappointed. I didn't have money to fight the

Little Castles case, but it was principle of the matter that they fired me for no reason. The attorney told me, "Maine is an at-will state. That means that any employee can be fired at any time for no reason." I didn't know that! So at that time, I was beginning to think I didn't have a chance to win my case! I think that Little Castles fired me because they didn't have a place for me because at that time, Little Castles was closing all of their stores. I think that's why they fired me!

I was unemployed, looking for a new job. I put some applications in but didn't hear from any companies. I put in an application at Brown Building Maintenance Service. They called me and asked me to come in for an interview. I went in and had the interview. It went great. They asked me if I would like to work for them. I said yes. They asked me if I could start the next day. I said yes. They introduced me to the manager of the job site I was going to. I met Clay. He was an okay guy. We talked, and he told me what I will be doing out at Med-pot. It was a general cleaning position. I had already done this type of work before. The next day, I went up to Med-pot and saw Clay. He introduced me to Sharon, the other worker there. We talked for a while, and he told Sharon to help me and to show me the building and what I would be doing. Sharon and I got along great. She showed me what I would be doing for the next eight hours, so I began to do my job. It was great. I had another job. The night went great. Sharon helped me that night. We took breaks, sat around, and talked, and the night was done. It was time to go home. Sharon asked me where I lived. I told her, and she said, "You do not live to far from me." She asked me to follow her. She lived not too far from me. After a month, we started to carpool. She drove one week, and I drove the next week. It worked out great.

I was putting my life back together, getting caught up with my bills, thinking about what just happened to me at Little Castles. My coworker and my manager were great! All Clay wanted was for us to do our job, and we did, so everything went well. Months went by. I felt good about my job! I was back to paying my bills. Things were good.

Then Sharon began to act funny. She began to boss me around. It wasn't bad, but I didn't like it! I was new to the job, so I listened to her. At Brown, there was always over time, so I worked some over time at other job sites. I started to meet other people in the company. One day I went in to work, and Clay said that the office wanted to talk to me, and I asked why. He said he didn't know, so I went to the office and talked with Clay's boss.

She said, "Sharon said that you sexually harassed her." I knew I didn't, but Clay's boss said, "We have to move you from Med-pot." I was so sad that I couldn't believe it! They put me on the floor crew. The manager of the floor crew was Ben. He was all right, so I began to go out with the floor crew. I got to know the guys. We went to job sites and did the floor. We did a lot of stripping and waxing the floor. That went on for months. Ben said that they needed a floor crew member to do the floors in the computer rooms. He asked me if I would like to do it. I said I would like to do it, so I went to Blink One Building at 170. That's where the computer rooms were. The floor crew member in the computer rooms met with me and showed me what to do. I liked it! I got to know the people in the computer rooms, so I kept the computer rooms clean and stripped and wax the floor eight hours a day. I loved it because on the floor crew, I didn't always get forty hours a week. It was Monday through Friday, then I began to get over time on the weekend with the floor crew. Things were going good. I had finally gotten a home and a good place to work. I was finally secure. Brown told me that they wanted me to go up to Blink One and help them out there, so I did and met the manager there. Her name was Tammy. She was great. She began to show me what she needed me to do, so I worked the computer rooms and helped out Tammy at night. She gave me a building at 150, and I helped to clean it. That was over time for me. That went on for months. Tammy was being reassigned, and Brown asked me if I would like to have Tammy's job as supervisor. I said yes, so I was the supervisor out at Blink One. It was great. I had a day porter and night porter and a night crew. I had about seventeen people for four buildings. I had a good crew. They showed up for work all the time. Rob was my day porter. He was good. He kept Blink One happy, so I never worried about the day crew at Blink One. Rob would call me if he had a problem, and I would go up and talk with Rob, go around, and talk to the contract people to see how things were going. Rob always knew what Blink One needed, so I would go back to the office or go home and get ready for the night crew. The night crew came in all the time. They knew their job and went to work. Most of the night crew were from Somalia and Ghana, Africa. They were good workers. I enjoyed it, so that went on for months.

Then my boss, John, was telling me that Brown was losing the contract at the McKinley Park. He said he wasn't sure, but he thought that might happen. He said that he would bring me over where he supervised with Blink One, so that did happen. Blink One was in a transition and was becoming Sandy Bank. Sandy Bank did let Brown keep some of the contract, but some they didn't keep like the buildings I had with Blink One, so I went over to where John was. I was acting manager with John. I met the night crew there. Some of my employees came with me, and others resigned.

I ran the crew, who all knew their job. They all came to work. I managed the building out there for months. John told me that he was leaving to go to a new job outside of Brown and said that he wanted me to be the supervisor out there! I met with John at the office and made it official that I was the supervisor out at Blink One. I was talking to John's boss, and he said that I was doing great with the company. I told him I enjoyed my job, so he told me what he was looking for out at Blink One, and that was to keep Blink One up! I said I would get the job done. I began to supervise out there. Blink One was a big operation. I had a day porter and night porter. I had about twenty employees. I supervised on any given day! I had a crew leader who helped me to get the job done! I always walked the buildings to supervise the work. My crew always did a great job. When we were caught up, I always let my worker relax some time. Out of four hours, they worked three hours. That's how good they were, and I think that's why they kept coming back because of how I managed the buildings. It was a great work environment. My boss Melody would stop by to see how things were going. Melody was very arrogant. She wasn't a very good supervisor. She was too bossy. I didn't like her, but she was my boss. She would tell me when she came over to the building they better be clean! She was very arrogant like she didn't respect the crew! The crew didn't like her when she came around. I told them, "When she comes around, just do your job because she has a job to do too." That went on for months. Everything was going good. Then one night, Melody came by and was talking to me, saying that Brown was losing the contract. I knew that because John told me that it was possible. Melody said that Blink One and First Union were being sold to Sandy Bank, and Brown didn't know if Sandy would honor the contract. Melody said, "Keep up the good work." I said okay. I didn't say anything to the crew because it wasn't a fact, so months went by. Melody called me to her office. I went, and she told me that Sandy wasn't honoring the contract, so all Blink One buildings were no longer Brown, but the main building was still Brown. I didn't manage that building, so Brown started to find my workers new positions in the company. I worked a supervisory job, but I got concerned that they didn't have a place for me. I was a supervisor, and I was worried about my future with the company. Months went by. Brown was downsizing, and I was cut. I had no job after all I did for the company. Brown didn't give me thanks for a job well done. There was no going-away gift, but I saw them give gifts to other supervisors, so yes, I was hurt. I knew I had to find new employment soon. I always saw a transportation van out. I always wanted to drive, so I filled out some applications for employment, but no one called. I saw a transportation company called Wheelchair Gwen. I filled out an application. They called me. I went in for an interview, and I meet a lady named Tracy. She asked me when I can start. I said, "Now." She said, "Come next week on Monday." They would train me for the job. I said thank you.

CHAPTER 12

I went into work on Monday. I met a girl named Jean. She knew I was coming. She said, "Hi, Brett." I also said hi. We went to the van, and she showed me how to inspect the van before putting it on the road. We did check the vehicle: the tire, the oil, the light, and the off-on switch. After that, I was cleared to drive. I got in the driver's seat, and she told me my first pickup. She gave me the address. I looked it up in the road map and started to drive there. When I got there, I knocked on the door. A lady came to the door and said, "He will be right out." I went to the van and got it ready for transport. The gentleman came out in a wheelchair. I helped him get in the van and tied him down. My trainer checked to see if the tie-downs were secured and that they were good and tight. I drove the client to his appointment, unloaded him, and took him in to his appointment. I gave him our card and told him when he was ready to come home, he should give us a call. My trainer said, "Brett, you are a natural." I smiled and went on with our day. I transported eight people that day and did the paperwork. I went back to the office, and she said, "I will see you tomorrow." I said thank you. I went home, and I was glad to be back employed again! I went back in the next day and did it all over again. It was great! I loved it. I was happy. My trainer worked with me all week. At the end of the week, she asked me if I was ready to go out by myself. I said, "I'm ready." She said she would tell Tracy that I was ready to go out next week on my own. Tracy approved it, and I went out the next week by myself and did what I did last week. After about three weeks, Tracy came to me and asked if I would like to keep the van at my house. I replied, "Yes, I would like to." She said that I could start taking the van home. I didn't know that other employees took their van home too. It was great that she trusted me. Tracy knew I was a homeowner and that I was responsible, so I started to take the van home after work.

I really loved my job. I was doing something that I wanted to do. I got to know other employees. We worked as a team. I met Tracy's mom. She was nice. I loved working there because I felt like I belonged. After what I went through on my other jobs, working is truly a ride-up and down. Things are not what they seem to be. People will say things on the job and start rumors, but you have to work through that. That's what makes you stronger. I went on with my life, paying my bills and my mortgage. After a year with the company, Tracy had a contract for adult day care with Robin House. We transported their clients to day care. One day Tracy asked me if I would like to transport some of their clients to day care in their company van. I said yes, and she said, "This is how it's going to work. It's going to be you and Jimmy." Jimmy was a driver I worked with at Wheelchair Gwen. Jimmy and I came in as usual, and we would go to Robin House and see a lady named Sue, who would give us our assignment. That's what we did for the morning, then after that, we would go back to our Wheelchair Gwen vans and drive for our company until 2:00 p.m. and then go back to Robin House and do an afternoon run to take the people whom we took in that morning back home. I liked it, so that's what we were doing for Wheelchair Gwen and Robin House.

In 1998. I wanted to buy a car, but at the time, I didn't know what kind of car I wanted. I kept thinking about it. One day I was driving the Robin bus. I was going down E. Summer Street, and I saw a car that looked like it was sitting there waiting for me. It was like telling me, "Come and get me!" I turned around and went to the car dealership and asked about the car. The dealer said that it was a good car and three people had looked at it too. He said that they couldn't get a finance for it. I told the guy that I had a great credit. He said, "Let's do the application." So we did, and he said that it would take a couple of days. It was okay with me. He said, "I will call you." I left and picked up my people from Robin House. That week, I got off work and went home. I did kind of forgot about the car because I had other things on my mind, so I wasn't thinking about it when my phone started to ring. I picked up and said, "Hi, who is this?" I didn't recognize the voice. The guy on the phone said, "It's me, the man from the car company."

I remembered. "Oh, hi, how are you doing?"

He replied, "Great! Brett, are you sitting down?" I said no and asked why. He said, "Come and get your car. You have been approved for the loan."

"That's great!"

He said, "Just come to the car dealership and sign some papers, and you can take the car home." It was a 1987 Mercedes-Benz 300 E. I was the second owner of the car. It was a very great time for me! I called a friend who worked at Robin House and asked him if he could take me to the car dealership to pick up my new car. He said yes, and he did! When we got to the car dealership, they had the car ready for me. It was washed and cleaned. I got in my car and drove home. I was very happy.

I didn't tell anyone at my company. I was like that because I didn't know anyone there, and I knew how people can be, so like I always did, I went to work and did my job. A couple of years went by, and no one at the company knew that I had my car. About two years into buying my car, I only had six payments left, so I showed the owner of the company my car. She was happy for me because she saw me progressing in my job while she knew the other employees were always asking for pay advance on their check. I never asked her for an advance. After I went back to work, I noticed Tracy started to change toward me. I didn't know why, but she was changing. I began to think why, and it came to me that Tracy got jealous of me because I was progressing in my job. It was like I never knew Tracy. It wasn't that bad, but I knew it wasn't the same, so I kept doing my job. At the time, we had Robin House transporting their clients, and I began to notice that Tracy was making me do the late runs. I was not used to doing that, but after I showed her my car, she changed, so there was nothing I could do. It was happening all over again. Every time I was doing something, helping myself on someone's job, something bad always happened. It seemed like they wanted me to work but didn't want me to progress! It seemed like people in all my jobs were like that. I began to think, was it because I was black? All the jobs I worked for, 92 percent of the employees were Caucasian. All my life I had to deal with that! It just seemed like it was never going to stop, but I didn't let it get to me, so I began to lie to Tracy. The other employees seemed like they were always getting off early, so I started telling Tracy that I was taking a class online and had to be off by 6:00 p.m. We came in at 6:00 a.m. then ended at 6:00 p.m., so it was a long day. Sometimes we might get there at 5:00 a.m. then ended at 9:00 p.m. I wanted to get off early too, but after showing Tracy my car, she changed to the point that she wanted to fire me. All of a sudden, she started to show no respect! But I have seen that all my life. It didn't bother me. I acted like I didn't know what was happening. I paid my car off, and I still have it with me today!

CHAPTER 13

Going in to 2000, work was going okay, but things seemed to change for me there because I showed the owner my car, and the other employees weren't making progress like me, a black man. But I had a job to do. I was on a mission! Given my background and being black, it was always a challenge, so I kept working. Tracy was moving her company from A Street to Oak Row Street in 2001, so we had a meeting about it. The job went on. Time had passed since I showed her my car. Things were a little better, so I acted like nothing happened, but I could feel things. I was bigger than that! I feel a person who is working should be able to buy what he wants! If you are working, you can do that! That was my way of thinking. A couple of years went by. It was January 2003. Tracy called a meeting and told us that she sold the company and that we should not worry about our jobs because the company she sold it to would honor her employees. She went on talking about other times, like how we made her proud, and she liked all of us for doing the job we did with her at Wheelchair Gwen. Five months later, the deal was done, and we went to the new company called West Ride Company. We met the new owners. They were nice, but I knew something wasn't right! I wasn't playing games. It was all real to me what was going on. I knew down the road that the new company would try to fire some of Tracy's employees because of salaries, and they would hire their new employees at a lower rate than they were paying us. A year went by. Some of Tracy's old employees began to see what I was seeing. Kent was a senior employee, and he didn't like what he was seeing. He walked out of the job, and that told all of us we had a problem. We talk to one another about Kent's walking out. Other employees also quit their jobs, so I began worry about my job. When I first went to the new company, I saw a man whom I thought I may have a problem with. The first thing that went through my mind was that this person was going to fire me! Seeing that Kent quit his job, I was feeling what the other employees were feeling. Thing just didn't feel right. A year went by. It was 2004. Things at the new company began to change. A lot of Tracy's employees began to quit, but I needed my job. At the time, I couldn't quit. I was forty-nine years old and a black man, and I knew it would be hard for me to get a job.

In October of 2004, I went in to work at 7:00 a.m., and I was told by the office staff that Mick wanted to talk to me. I was wondering what he wanted to talk to me about. I couldn't work till I talked to Mick, so I sat in his office till Mick came in. Mick came in at 9:00 a.m. and said he would talk to me soon. About 9:30 a.m., he called me into his office and said that a girl said I was trying to sexually assault her. I said I didn't do that. Mick said the girl said that I did! The man whom I thought would fire me did fire me! Mick said, "But I will give you a good resume."

I told him, "Mick, I didn't do that."

He said, "You probably didn't, but we do not want a lawsuit on us, that's why we have to let you go." That was the same person I was talking about early in my story. I knew he was going to fire me when I first saw him, so I was fired. No indication, nothing, just fired. I went home. I was hurt. My whole life was in front of me. I worked hard to keep my job, but the same thing kept happening! I kept getting fired! I began to wonder, was I getting fired because I was black? All my jobs seemed like that. I always did a good job where I was working, but for some reason, I kept getting fired. At the time, I had a really good girlfriend. Her name was Sophia. She supported me through it. She did everything she could do, but she knew I was hurt and mad!

I began to make plans for my life. My girlfriend Sophia was very nice to me. I met her at a voting booth. I just went in to vote, and she was the coordinator of the voting station. It was like she fell in love with me at first sight. Sophia was great! We began to date. I was telling her about me, and she was telling me about her. I was telling Sophia about my mother and how I grew up and when I was in jail for nothing. I told her that my mother never showed me love and that she wished she never had me. It was always out of anger. I also told Sophia, "Before I met you, I took three other girlfriends over to meet my mother. I was still trying to be a son in spite of everything my mother put me through. On three different occasions, they all told me, 'Brett, when you left to go get your mother some pop and candy, she told me that you don't like to work!' I couldn't understand it because at the time, I had been in my home for eighteen years and just bought a Mercedes-Benz a couple of years ago. Sophia, my mother was always stabbing me in my back, and I couldn't understand why she would do that to me."

Sophia said, "I would like to meet your mother."

"Yeah, I'm going to take you over there to meet her." I took Sophia over to meet my mother, never thinking that my mother would actually tell Sophia after everything I had been through with her. I was buying my home! I was secure. Sophia told me, "Brett, when you left to take your sister for a ride in your car, your mother told me that you don't like to work. I was thinking about what you told me about your other girlfriends, and you were right!" I was disappointed. Sophia could see I was disappointed, so that was when I made my up mind to divorce my family! I had enough! I liked Sophia a lot. She was just what I needed—a friend. She showed me a lot of attention.

CHAPTER 14

Two days later, I got a call from a social worker. His name was Andrew. I answered the phone, and Andrew said hi. I replied, "Hi, Andrew."

He said, "A Russian guy wanted to talk to you about a transportation job."

I said, "Okay, when does he want to talk to me?"

"As soon as possible."

"I can talk to him today." Andrew said he would call me back. I was so excited! I called my girlfriend and told her the good news. She told me when one door closes, another one opens. Sophia was so happy for me. I began to feel good again. I was so hurt because it was so unfair for West Ride to fire me. The next day, Andrew called me back and said that the Russian guy wanted to meet me that day. I immediately agreed. Andrew asked me if he could give the Russian guy my number. I said yes. Andrew didn't know that I just got fired, so about an hour went by, and the phone started to ring. I picked it up, and a Russian guy was on the phone.

He said, "Can I speak with Brett?"

I answered, "I'm Brett."

"Hi, my name is Akim." I said hi. He asked me if he could come by and pick me up. I said, "Yes, you can." I gave him directions to my home. I was so excited. It was like a miracle. My prayer was answered! Akim found my house. I came out to meet him. He got out of the driver's side of the new wheelchair van, and I said, "I can drive." When I got into the van, he said, "Brett, I need you to go a to a nursing home called Rose Dale." He didn't tell me where it was, but I knew, so I started to drive to Rose Dale. We got there. Throughout the trip, he was watching me, and he knew that he had an "experienced driver." We went inside the nursing home and went to the room where the client was waiting for us. We introduced ourselves as First Ride Transportation, and the first trip I had with my new company was the lady who showed the curtains on the "Buy Is Now." Her name was Emma. I was so happy and proud of the new company. We transported the client to her appointment and dropped her off and told her to give us a call when she was ready to go back. We thanked her. I could tell that Akim was very happy. He said, "Let's go get lunch." We went to a Greek restaurant and had lunch and talked. I told Akim that I knew the whole city and the surrounding neighborhoods and suburbs. He loved it. We went back to pick up our client and took her back to the nursing home.

Akim and I went to another client's home and picked her up. I could see that Akim was happy because he knew he had a driver for his company, and I was happy because I knew I had finally found security on my job. The day went like this. I picked up clients, and Akim was always on the phone speaking Russian. The day ended. Akim said that the next day we were going to Paul City to pick up a wheelchair van for him. I said, "Okay, Akim." He took me home and said, "Thank you, Brett, you did a great job for us. See you in the morning."

I replied, "Thanks, Akim, see you in the morning."

I was so happy because I was back to work, and I had security. I went into my house and knew that all my dreams had come true! I fixed dinner, and I had a great sleep that night. Before this job, I couldn't sleep because I just got fired three days ago. The next day, Akim picked me up at 8:00 a.m., and we went to Paul City to pick up his wheelchair van. Akim picked out the van he wanted. It was a minivan. Akim signed the papers, and we were off. We went to have lunch and talk. Akim said, "Brett, Andrew told me a lot about you." He said he liked what he heard. I said thank you. Akim said, "We are a small company now, but we want to be a big company."

I said, "I would like to help you be a big company." We continued to talk. We still had people to pick up, so Akim gave me some runs to pick up and the times to pick them up. I had three runs that day. I ran the route and picked them up. Akim would check up on me to see how things were going. I told him, "Great, Akim, because this what I do." When the day ended, Akim called me. "Brett, you can take the van home." I said thank you. Akim said, "See you in the morning." I said okay. At that time, the owner of the company trusted me with the company van after two days of meeting me. It was a 2004 Ford van. That made me feel good and secured!

The next day, we did it all over again. Akim was very nice to me. He gave me gift cards to restaurants. No one had ever done this for me! I felt respected and appreciative of everything he did for me. That day ended too. On my third day on the job, Akim called me and said that the client was very happy with our company. That was great news. Akim said, "Brett, I am glad to meet you. You are doing a great job for our company." It was very exciting for me to hear this because I was just wrongly fired four days ago! That day ended too. Akim called me. "Brett, I'll see you in the morning. Have a good night."

I replied, "You too, Akim."

The next day came. Akim had a list of clients for me to pick up. He gave the list, and I told Akim, "Don't worry."

He said, "Brett, with you, I don't have to worry." That was great for me because Akim respected me. The other companies always tried to control me. I began to run the route, and I picked up all the clients Akim gave me. That day ended too. I really felt good about my job. For the first time I felt respected and appreciated. Time went on. Six months went by. Akim asked me if I knew any driver. I said yes. Akim asked me, "Brett, can you see if he would like to work with us?" I said I will call him that night to see if my friend would like to work with us. The new company was growing fast. Akim just bought a brand-new ambulance. He was so happy, and I was happy for him. I knew that I had found a job that I can feel comfortable about, where I was respected and where I can make plans for my life. That night, I called a friend. His name was Mark. I asked him if he was interested in working with the new company I was working at.

Mark said, "Brett, if you are working there, I know that it's a good company!" He added, "I would like to work with the company." I said great, so I started to tell him about the company. Mark said, "Brett, when we worked at Wheelchair Gwen, we knew the city then and still know the city."

I said to Mark, "That's just what we need to get the new company on its feet! I will call you tomorrow and tell you when you could meet Akim."

"Great, Brett!"

"Talk to you tomorrow."

The next day, I talked to Akim and told him that I have a driver for us. Akim was happy. He said, "Brett, can I trust your friend? I said yes. Akim asked, "When can I meet him?"

"I would call him now."

Mark and Akim talked. Akim had just bought a new wheelchair van, and he hired Mark that same day. I was happy to have Mark on board. Akim asked me, "Brett, will Mark be able to start tomorrow?"

"Yes, no problem."

Akim said, "Great. I will work with Mark for a couple of days."

I told him, "Akim, Mark can go out on his own."

"Okay, Brett."

The next day came. We met at my house, and Akim said we should follow him. Mark and I got in my van and followed Akim to where he kept his vans. Mark got into the van. Akim gave him his route to run and gave me a route to run. The day went off without a hitch. At the end of the day, we met Akim, and he said thanks to me and Mark. Akim said, "Take the van back and take Mark home, and I will see you guys in the morning." I said, "Thanks. See you in the morning."

The next day, Mark met me at my house at 7:00 a.m. Akim showed up about 7:30 a.m. He asked us how we were doing. We said great. Akim gave us our route and gave the keys to Mark, and I took him to where the van was.

"Have a great day, Mark."

"You too, Brett," Mark replied. We went and ran the routes Akim gave us. Mark and I talked during the day. He said, "Brett, this is great. I already like this job!" I said great. Everybody was happy. Akim called me that day. "I'm thinking about letting Mark take the van home." I said Mark would take good care of the van. Akim said, "Thanks, Brett." Mark called me that day and said that Akim called him and said he could take the van home. I was happy for Mark!

Akim was trying to see if he could trust Mark with the van. I knew he could, but I knew he had to find out for himself. That day ended. Akim called us that day and said he would see us tomorrow. He said, "Have a good night." We said okay and that we would see him in the morning.

Mark and I went home.

CHAPTER 15

The next day, Akim called me at 7:30 a.m. and said that he called Mark and gave him his schedule and told me he would call me back. I said okay. Mark called me and said Akim called him and gave him his trip list. Mark said he had six runs for the day. That means twelve runs for the day, transporting and return trips. I said I talked to Akim too. He said he would call me back. I told Mark to have a great day and I would talk to him later in the day. He said, "Okay, Brett." Akim called me about an hour later and gave me my schedule. I had four runs for the day. That means eight runs for the day, transporting and return trips.

That day was coming to an end. All the runs were done for the day. Mark called me and said Akim called him and said he could go home. I said, "Great, Mark, have a great night, and see you in the morning."

Akim called at the end of the day and said that a guy was interested in driving for us. "He said that he worked with you, Brett."

I asked, "What is his name?"

"Ron."

I told Akim I knew who he was talking about. He asked me if he was reliable. I really didn't like Ron, but I told Akim he could rely on Ron. I also told him, "If you hire Ron, he could come right in and get in the van and start transporting the same day."

"He could?"

I said yes. Akim said he would think about it.

I had been at this job with the new company for about six months, and the business was growing. I was glad to be a part of the new company. It was great for me. No more stress, and I could start making real plans for my life and home, and so I did!

About three weeks later, Akim called me again and asked me that he was thinking about hiring Ron. I knew that Ron would be good for the company. I told Akim Ron was a man who could come in and start making runs for the company. Akim told me, "My company is growing because of you, Brett! My clients have been calling me about you, and how kind you are and nice and always helping them and making sure that they are safe in their transport and that you are a great driver!"

I said, "Wow! Thanks, Akim, for telling me about that. That made me feel good." That day came to an end. Mark called and said, "Akim said I could go home."

I said, "Mark, have a great night. See you in the morning."

He said, "Great. You too, Brett."

The next day, Akim called me and said he needed me to ride with him so he could pick up another wheelchair van. He said, "We are a little slow today, Brett. I called Mark and gave him his runs for the day." Akim came to my house and picked me up. He took me to breakfast, and he was telling me about the company. He was telling me about how he and his family saw the business growing and was glad that Akim met me.

Akim said, "You are everything Andrew said you would be. My family wants to meet you!"

I replied, "I would like that." After eating breakfast, we went to pick up the wheelchair van. After that, Akim did what he had to do. I got into his car and drove it back to where he kept his vans, and Akim drove me back to my house and gave me my runs for the day. It was a slow day. Mark called me at the end of the day and asked me how was my day. I said, "Great, Mark." I told him that Akim just bought another wheelchair van.

Mark said, "He did?"

"The company is growing."

He said, "That's great! I know Akim was glad he met you, Brett!"

Mark new that there was security on the job. I told Mark that Akim was thinking about hiring Ron.

He said, "What?"

I said, "Yeah."

Mark knew Ron from when we worked at Wheelchair Gwen. Mark said that Ron could jump right in and start to drive right away. I said, "I know." Mark said he didn't really like Ron, but if he could help the company grow, why not?

That day ended too.

The next day, Akim called me and said to meet him at 285 at 8:00 a.m., so I did. When I got there, Akim was talking with Andrew. They said, "Hi, Brett."

I replied, "Hi, guys." We went into Andrew's office, and we began to talk. Akim was telling Andrew he was glad to meet me. Andrew said, "I knew Brett would be good for the company." We talked a little longer, and Andrew had to leave. Akim and I were talking, and he said he hired Ron. "Great! He can come right in and start to work," I commented.

"I hired him because of you, Brett!"

"He will not let the company down," I replied.

Akim said, "I have him on the schedule for tomorrow."

"Great!"

Akim said, "Brett, I have ordered a new ambulance. It will be here in two weeks."

I said, "Wow, Akim, the company is growing."

"Because of you, Brett, your experience and your manner with our clients!"

"Thank you, Akim."

He gave me my schedule. "Brett, you have a slow schedule today. Go home and relax. I will call you later." I said okay and went home to relax. I knew that I had a great boss and a great job.

I called Mark and asked him how his day was going. He said, "Good. I have made the runs Akim gave me for the morning. My next pickup is at 11:30 a.m., and I'm at home eating."

I said, "Mark, this is a great job."

"Brett, I'm glad you told me about Akim."

I said, "I knew you would like it!" I told Mark that Akim hired Ron. He said, "He did?"

"Yeah, he did that good because you and I know that Ron could get right in and start the job."

Mark said, "It makes it easy for us. It's not like it's a hard job because, Brett, me and you know this is nothing like the Tracy job, Wheelchair Gwen. She had lots of runs and about fifteen drivers. At the new company, First Ride Transportation, it is up and coming."

"Yep, and with Ron, it will get better. Okay, Mark, talk to you later. Have a good day."

"You too, Brett."

Akim called me at about 11:30 a.m. and said, "Brett, I have some Russians for you to pick up." I said okay, and he gave me my schedule. I ran my schedule for that day, and at the end of the day, Akim called me and said, "The Russian people said that they like you, Brett!"

I said, "That's great, Akim."

"Have a good night. Ron will start tomorrow."

I replied, "Okay, Akim, you have a great night too. See you tomorrow."

Akim was showing me respect because he knew that I have the experience that he was looking for. He called me the next day at about 10:00 a.m. and said that he had given Mark and Ron their schedule for the day. Akim said he wanted me to ride with him that day. I said okay, so Akim came and picked me up at my house and said, "Brett, the company is growing fast!"

"That's great, Akim."

Then Akim began to tell me what he was doing. "I am going to buy another ambulance, and in a month, I am going to buy a wheelchair van, so I am going to put an ad in the newspaper to find another driver."

I said, "Akim, your company is really growing."

"Because of you, Brett!" Akim said that his family wanted to meet me. I said okay. Akim said, "I will bring them to your house tomorrow when I bring you your new uniforms."

"Okay, Akim, I look forward to meeting them." Akim took me to lunch, and we talked some more. I knew Akim liked me and was glad to meet me. I was happy to meet Akim. The company was still young. Akim had been in business for about eight months, and he already had three wheelchair vans and two ambulances and was going to buy another wheelchair van and an ambulance. After lunch, Akim took me back home and said, "Brett, I just need you to pick up some Russians, the same people you picked up before." It was 12:30 p.m. Akim said it was my only run for the day. I said okay.

Akim said, "Pick them up at 1:30 p.m. and wait on them and take them back home, and then you can go home."

I said, "Thank you, Akim."

I called Mark and asked him how his day was going. He said, "Brett, this is great! Brett, Akim called me just this morning and gave me my schedule. I have six runs for today." I said cool. Mark asked me if I saw Ron. I said no, but Akim said Ron was on the road. Mark said that was good. I said, "Have a good day."

"You too, Brett."

I said, "Talk to you later." I picked up the Russians and took them to their appointments and waited on them and took them back home about 3:30 p.m., and then I went home for the day.

The next day, about nine thirty that morning, I was outside and saw a car pull in my driveway. I didn't know the lady who was in the car. She looked at me, and I looked at her, then I saw Akim pull up. He had a man in his van. Akim got out of his van, and the lady got out of her car. Akim said, "Brett, this is my mother and this is my father."

I said, "Hi, I'm glad two meet both of you."

They said, "Akim has said a lot of good things about you, Brett, and we wanted to meet you for ourselves." Akim's mother said, "What a nice house you have, Brett."

"Thank you."

Akim's dad shook my hand. "It's nice to meet you, Brett."

"Thank you, sir."

Akim said his father was on dialysis. "Brett, I want you to transport my father to and from dialysis." I said okay. Akim's parents said that Akim told them that I got them some really good drivers. I said, "Yes, these guys can really do the job." Akim's father said, "That's what we need, and we are really glad we met you, Brett!"

"Thank you!" I was so happy that I had really found a workplace where I can work and just do my job! After meeting Akim's family, Akim gave me my schedule. "I will call you later, Brett."

I said, "Okay, and thank you for everything."

CHAPTER 16

I called **Mark and asked him** how his day was going. He said, "Great, Brett, I really like the way this van runs. It's not like Tracy's vans."

"I know."

Mark asked, "Have you seen Ron?'

"No, but I will see you and him today because Akim wants me to give you and him your uniforms."

Mark said, "Brett, that's great!"

I told Mark, "Meet me at my house at noon, and I will give you your uniform."

Mark said, "See you at your house at noon."

"Okay, see you then."

I went home and ate lunch. Mark came by, and I gave him his uniforms. We talked for a little bit, and Mark said he had to go and pick up his client. I said, "Okay, have a great day, Mark."

"You too, Brett."

I called Ron and asked him to meet me at Saint Mary's Hospital at 2:00 p.m. "I have your uniforms." He said okay, so I met Ron at 2:00 p.m. at Saint Mary's Hospital. That was the first time I saw him. He smiled and said, "Hi, Brett."

"Hey, Ron, how do you like the job?"

He said, "Brett, I love it! Akim has a new van. He has great clients. I like it."

"Great! Akim wants us to wear our uniforms every day."

Ron said cool and put on his uniform. I said, "Have a great day, Ron."

"You too, Brett."

I went and picked up the Russians and took them to their appointment and waited on them then took them back home. That was my only run for that day.

Things were going good for the company. The next day, Akim called me and said his company was getting bigger. I said, "That's great, Akim." Akim had two ambulances and had to go interview two EMT drivers for the position. I said okay. He gave me my schedule, and I ran my schedule. I had a good day. I didn't talk to Mark or Ron that day. When the day ended, I went home. It's about a year into the new job. When I met Akim, he had one wheelchair van and no ambulance. Now he had three wheelchair vans and two ambulances. Akim called me that day and said he hired two EMT drivers and that they had to take a test to get certified, then he could put them on the road. Akim was looking for a business building to keep his ambulances in, so he took me with him to look at some buildings. He had seen some, but they weren't what he was looking for. We went to another place, and Akim seemed to like the building. It had an office space, it had a big bay to keep the ambulances, and it had a bedroom for the EMS ambulance employees to sleep and shower. It also had a room where the employees could relax and a big parking lot so the employees could park their car. Akim said, "This is just what I have been looking for. This is going to be our new home, Brett." I was glad for Akim and for me too. He said, "Brett, you can go home, and I will talk to you tomorrow."

"Thanks, Akim. Talk to you tomorrow. Have a great day."

"You too, Brett."

Akim was really showing me respect, so I went home. I called Mark and asked him how his day was going. He said, "Brett, I love this job. It's not hard. I like the people I pick up and the Russians!"

I said, "Great! Have a great day."

"You too, Brett."

I enjoyed my day off. Akim called me later that day and said, "Brett, tomorrow I want you to meet the EMT drivers that I hired."

"Okay."

He said, "Our company is really growing. Come to the new office tomorrow at 9:00 a.m." Akim said he would like to have breakfast with me.

I said, "See you at 9:00 a.m."

I had a great day off. I went to the office the next day and met with Akim. We ate breakfast, and after eating, he introduced me to the employees. Akim told them that I started the company with him and his family. They were glad to meet me. I could see the company growing. My employment was secured. For the first time in a long time, I was pretty much always intimidated in my other jobs, but in life, only the strong survive! At that time, Akim pretty much had Mark and Ron running the schedule for the week. Akim wanted me to be around him. He liked me not just as an employee but as a friend too! I liked that. Meeting his family made it like a personal relationship, which was great. The year 2004 came to an end. It was a great year for me and the new company.

CHAPTER 17

Going in to 2005, I had been thinking for a long time about my family. In 2005, my sister Judy said she needed a car to get to work, so I surprised her one day and bought her a car. I told Judy that she could pay me once a month for her car. She was so excited. She said, "I will pay you once a month."

I told Judy, "I will put you on my car insurance, and next month, you can pay the car insurance." She said okay. Judy got in her new car with a big smile on her face and tears in her eyes and drove off. That same day, Judy called me and was so excited she told her girlfriends what her brother had done for her. She let me talk to her friends, and they said they wished they had a brother like me! That made me feel good. I told them that I was happy to do that for my sister. A month later, Judy didn't call me or pay me the first payment! I called Judy, and she said, "I'm going to pay you!"

I said, "Okay, but after thirty days, there will be a late charge on it, twenty-six dollars" She ended up paying me, but it seemed like she had an attitude! A month went by, and Judy called me and said that she would get her own car insurance. I said, "Judy, we agreed that you would pay the next car insurance payment."

She said, "No, I'm going to get my own car insurance."

"Judy, that's going to put me in a bad financial situation."

"Nah, it's cheaper for me!"

"Judy, we agreed on how we're going to pay for the car insurance. Now you are reneging on me?" Judy didn't live up to her word. I had a chance to do something good for my sister. I thought that was a great thing to do for my sister, but she was reneging on me! Then she started to treat me like I was a stranger, and she got her car insurance. That put me in a bind. About six months passed, and Judy called me and said, "The car broke down. I'm not going to pay you for the broken-down car!" She had someone work on it, and they messed it up.

I told her, "Judy, that was your choice, not mine. You still have to pay for the car." She was mad and had an attitude! Eventually she paid me for the car, but with everything she put me through, I'll never do that again for her! With everything that I had been through with my brothers and my sisters and my mother, I decided to separate myself from my family! I love my family, but I just couldn't keep going on this way. I was hurt. I was by myself with no support from my family all these years. No one stood up for me! I left the door open for them to call or write me, but no one ever got in contact with me. I did everything a son could and a brother could. I will not look back. I have my whole life in front of me.

Going into the new year with Akim was great. I have been through so much with jobs and family. It was nice to be somewhere where I felt secured.

Going into the workweek of the new year was just like the last year—great! Akim called me and asked me how my New Year was. I said, "It was great. I'm glad to be working with your company."

"I'm glad I met you, Brett!"

I said, "Thank you, Akim." He gave me my schedule, and I went on with my day. I called Mark and asked him how was his New Year. He said, "Great, Brett, how was yours?"

"Great too."

Mark said, "Akim called me this morning and gave me my schedule. Brett, with Ron, the schedule isn't that bad, but I see that it's getting busy."

I agreed. "Yep, it's going to get busy. Okay, Mark, have a good day."

"Talk to you later, Brett. You have a good day too."

"Okay, Mark, bye."

I ran my schedule that day. Akim called me and said he hired another driver. I said, "Wow, Akim, the company is really growing." He said that he ordered another wheelchair van. I said, "That's great!"

Akim said, "Until the new van comes, we are going to share your van with the new driver."

I said, "Okay, Akim."

"Brett, when you are off, the new driver will come to your house and park his car at your house and drive your van for the day, and when he gets off, he will bring the van back to you house."

I said, "That's great, Akim." He said the driver's name was Scott. I said okay.

A week went by. Akim called that weekend. "The new driver starts this week, and he will be driving your van." I said okay.

"Brett, Scott will be at your house at 8:00 a.m. Monday. I want you to ride with me this week."

I replied, "Okay, Akim." I had a good weekend. Monday came. I hadn't met Scott yet, so 8:00 a.m. came, and a car pulled up in my driveway. A guy got out of the car and asked, "Can I speak to Brett?"

"I'm Brett."

"My name is Scott. I'm the new driver Akim hired."

I said, "I was waiting for you to come by. Akim told me about you. Welcome to the company. I think that you are going to like your job." We talked a little bit. Scott said, "Akim told me that you started the company with him and his family."

"Yes, I did. Scott, we are a young company, but we are growing."

He said, "Akim gave me my schedule."

I said, "That's my baby! Here are the keys."

Scott smiled. "I will take good care of your baby."

"Have a great day, Scott." Scott got his things out of his car and put them into the van. I told Scott, "You have to do a vehicle check every morning." I showed him how to do it and the paperwork for the vehicle check. "After you do the vehicle check, sign the vehicle checklist and throw it in with your run sheet." Scott said okay. He did the vehicle checklist, and he said, "Everything checked out. I'm good to go." He got in the van and went to run his schedule. It was about 8:45 a.m. Akim called me and said he was going to come and pick me up at 10:00 a.m. I said okay. It was great the way Akim was running his company, so I relaxed a little bit. At about 9:45 a.m., Akim pulled up and said, "Good morning, Brett."

"Good morning, Akim." He brought coffee and donuts for us.

He asked me what I thought of Scott. I said, "I like him. He's an older driver. That's good for the company. Someone you can depend on." Akim and I talked a little and drunk our coffee and ate some donuts. Akim said, "Brett, I want you to meet my grandmother."

I said, "Okay, Akim." He said that he wanted me to help him move something for his grandmother. I said okay, so we went to where his grandmother lived. Akim introduced me to his grandmother. She didn't speak English, but by that time, I had transported a lot of Russian and Ukrainian people, so I was used to it. Akim translated. He talked with his grandmother a little. His mother came by. I liked her, and she liked me. It was like family. It really was. The reason we went over to his grandmother's house was to move some furniture for her, then Akim's mother went and got lunch for us. While eating lunch, Akim talked to his mother and grandmother, and then he took me back home and said, "Thanks, Brett, for helping me to move the furniture for my grandmother."

I said, "Akim, you can count on me!"

"Brett, have a good day, and I will talk to you tomorrow."

"Talk to you tomorrow, Akim." At about 5:00 p.m. that day, Scott pulled back in my driveway. He washed the van and cleaned it up for me. I asked him how his day went. He said, "It went great, Brett, and your van ran good!"

"You will be driving it until Akim gets a new van."

Scott said, "Brett, it's been a long day. I'm going home, and I will see you in the morning."

"Scott, have a good evening." I didn't talk to Mark that day, but I will talk to him the next day and let him know how the new driver did on his first day out with the company.

The next day, Scott came by at 8:00 a.m. to pick up the van. "Brett, I look forward to this day. I like the people I picked up yesterday."

I said, "Great! That's what we need to hear." He got in the van and went off to run his schedule. It's my day off, so I did something around the house. It just felt great to finally find a secure employment. It makes me feel really great! Around lunchtime, Akim called me and asked if I was busy. I said no. He asked me if I could ride with him that day. I said I could, so Akim came by about 12:30 p.m. He took me to lunch, and he was telling me about how the company was growing. He had already hired four EMT ambulance drivers, two medics, and two basic. Akim said he was ordering two more ambulances, and they would be in about two weeks. "Brett, since I hired you, the company has continued to grow. With the wheelchair drivers that you brought to the company and the EMS drivers I hired from the ad I put in the newspaper, the Ambulance Division is really growing. I'm looking forward to launching the Ambulance Division off next week because they are still being certified to get their license to drive an ambulance." We talked some more, and I said, "I had done a lot before I met you, Akim."

Akim asked me, "Brett, what did you before you began to transport?" I told him.

CHAPTER 18

I told Akim, "I started with Pizza Talk in 1988, and I started off as a dough master, and I was promoted to shift manager. The manager of the store was great to work with. His name was Doug. Doug helped me a lot. He taught me how to run the store and how to do the paperwork, how to check the inventory and everything I needed to know about the shift manager job.

"So I began to open and close the store with other shift managers. It was a great experience."

Akim asked, "Brett, it seemed like a great job for you."

"It was, Akim."

"Why did you leave?"

I answered, "I was fired for doing my job! My old assistant manager Tony knew that Doug fired me. Tony left the company and went to Little Castles to manage over there. The pay was better at Little Castles, and the opportunities were endless. Tony called me and said, 'Brett, I will get you a job over here,' and he did!" I told Akim that two days went by, and Tony called me and said I had the assistant manager position! Tony said that the opportunities were endless and that he was talking to his supervisor about me and said what a great worker I was when we were at Pizza Talk together and that he might be able to get me a store with Little Castles.

"Tony told me, 'So, Brett, you will start in one week, but first you have to go to the corporation's office to fill out the paperwork.' So I went to Little Castles Corporation and met the staff and filled out the application and took a math test and talked to Tony's supervisor. His name was Daniel. He was a nice guy. Daniel told me that there was a great opportunity there for me to run a store with Tony. He said, 'Tony told me a lot about you and how you ran the store at Pizza Talk.' I said thank you. Daniel asked me, 'When can you start?' I said, 'I can start tomorrow or when the company needs me to start.'

"'I have already talked to Tony. I can start you next week. I will talk to Tony and tell him that you will start next Monday.' I said, 'Thank you, Daniel.' At the corporation's office that day, they bought me lunch. I ate lunch at the office. They made me feel welcome, so after all of that, I left and called Tony and told him how it went. Tony said Daniel called him and said I seemed to be the guy for them, and he told Daniel I was the right guy for them. Tony asked me, 'What size of uniform do you wear?' I said large. He said, 'Okay, I will have some uniforms for you on Monday.'"

"Tony said, 'Brett, go home. I will call you.' I said, 'Okay, Tony, have a great day.'"

I told Akim I then started with Little Castles.

"I was at Tony's store for about one year. I couldn't imagine being trained by any other manager! Tony was sharp when it came to managing a store. It was a little different from Pizza Talk, but basically the same paperwork, inventory, cash, scheduling, labor, etc., so I got the handle of operation. Before you know it, I was opening and closing the store, and I was making the schedule, and I was running the operation in the store. I got to meet the employees, and they were very nice. We worked together as a team. I got to meet the assistant managers. I was an assistant manager in training to be a manager. After one year, I opened the store one morning, and Tony called me and asked me how things were going. I said, 'Great, Tony, thanks for giving me this opportunity!'

"'Brett, I'm coming to the store. I have good news for you.' So I said, 'Tony, see you in a little.' Tony came to the store, and as usual, he looked around to see if the store was clean, but he knew that I was opening the store, and it's running great. Tony looked at me with a big smile on his face and said, 'Brett, the store at Land, they're going to fire the manager there, and I put your name in for the manager position at the Land Store.'

"That's great news, Tony," I said.

Tony said that he will know later that week, but Daniel said that I would be the best manager for that store! I said wow. Tony left, and I ran my shift and went home for the evening.

"The next day, I had to close. I went in at 3:00 p.m. to 11:00 p.m. Tony came by about 7:00 p.m. and asked how was business. I said good. Tony said, 'Brett, I want to talk to you.' I said okay, so we went outside of the store. He said, 'Brett, you got the store.' I was so happy. Tony was happy for me because he knew my wife had left me because I told him. Tony said, 'I will take you over to the store tomorrow to meet the employees.' I said, 'That's great!' Tony left, and I went back inside to run and close the store.

"The next day, I met Tony at our Rose Road Store at 10:00 a.m., and we went over to my store. I had never been there before. The first thing I noticed was the store wasn't very clean, and the employees all had long hair, and their uniforms were really dirty. Tony introduced me to the employees at the store. I walked around to check behind the make table and walk-in. The food wasn't dated! The walk-in wasn't clean, and the temperature wasn't at the FDA recommendation of 41 degrees Fahrenheit or lower, 36 degrees Fahrenheit. I saw why Little Castles had to make a change. Tony and I left, and he said, 'Brett, go do your thing.' I said, 'I will. I am learning from the best—you, Tony. I will make you proud!' The next day, I went over as the official manager of the Land Store and got to work. I helped clean the store. I talked to the employees, and they told me that they didn't like the old manager. They smoke, and they didn't put out a great product. That's why their sales were down, and that's why Little Castles was considering closing their store. They asked me, 'Brett, can you help us?' I said, 'Yes, I can. I will help bring back the Land Store.' I brought the store sales back up to 85 percent. About three months after I brought the store back up, Little Castles came in the middle of dinner rush and closed the store without any warning. No consideration for the employees or customers or me as the manager."

Akim asked, "Brett, what did you do after that?"

"Little Castles made me an area supervisor. I had three stores to supervise. It was great!"

Akim said, "Brett, it seemed like a great position."

"It was, Akim, but after about three months, a female employee said that I sexually harassed her. They didn't investigate the act. They believed the female employee and not me, the area supervisor! Little Castles fired me, Akim.

"Then I started working for a company named Brown Building Maintenance Service. I started as a general cleaner, then I was promoted to manager. Years went by. It was great working there, then Brown lost the contract, so I had to start working split shifts to get my hours. it didn't work out.

"Then, Akim, that's when I got into transporting in 1997. I started with a company named Wheelchair Gwen. In the early '70s, I drove a cab, so I did know the city back then. When I went through training and started transporting, it was great there. I enjoyed transporting people and the facilities I went to. In 2000, the owner sold the company to a company called West Ride. Before we went to the new company, Tracy, the owner of Wheelchair Gwen, had a meeting with us, and she told us that nothing was going to change, not our salary or our hours. She said she made sure of that before she signed the contract. We all went to the new company the next week and met the new owners. They were nice. They had minivans for us to transport in, so we started to transport for West Ride. Tracy had given them the contract that we had, so we were transporting the same people. We were transporting with Wheelchair Gwen and their people too. After about six months, some of the Wheelchair Gwen employees started to leave. After a year, things started to change, and I got concerned about my job! I started wondering if I will be able to pay my mortgage or if I will get fired. So eventually, Akim, I did get fired. I was accused of sexual harassment by a female client.

"Then, Akim, that's when I met you."

Akim said, "Brett, you have done a lot."

"Yes, I did, Akim." We finished our lunch, and Akim said, "Brett, I will take you back home," so he did. When we arrived, he said, "Have a good day off, Brett. I will talk to you tomorrow."

I said, "You have a good day too." Akim left, and I just relaxed the rest of the day.

The next day, Akim wanted me to ride with him a lot. I was not sure why, but Akim was always respectful to me! I never questioned a thing. Akim had Mark and Scott running the schedule. It wasn't that busy at the time. I enjoyed it. Akim picked me up at my home, and I rode with him. He told me that he was launching the Ambulance Division next week because all of his drivers were certified. "Akim, that's great!" He was very happy. I was happy for him too. We rode to some facilities Akim was hoping that he could get for his Ambulance Division. He said, "We are talking with them now, Brett."

"Do you think we might get them?"

He replied, "We have our Wheelchair Division in them, so we have a good chance of getting a contract with them." Akim added, "We just got a contract with one of the facilities and hope to get more."

"That's good, Akim!" I was so happy to be with this company! I had no worries, so we went to lunch. After that, Akim gave me my schedule. He wanted me to pick up some Russians and take them back home. Akim took me back home, and I ran my schedule, and I finally had a chance to call Mark and see how his week was going. He said, "Great, Brett. I haven't heard from you in a while. Where have you been?"

"I have been riding with Akim. He's getting ready to launch his Ambulance Division next week."

"Brett, I know Akim is glad he met you."

"Yep, I am glad to meet Akim too."

Mark said that he liked the job.

"Great, Mark, have you heard from Ron or Scott?"

"No, Brett, I haven't heard from them, but I did see Ron and Scott transporting."

I said, "That's good. Well, Mark, I will talk to you later. Have a great day."

"You too, Brett."

CHAPTER 19

I got off that day. After one year with Akim, the company was really growing. The next day, Akim called me to come to his office. I went to the office to see what he needed. When I got there, I saw Akim with some people whom I hadn't seen before. I went over where Akim was, and he introduced me to his EMS drivers. He was launching his Ambulance Division the next week. Akim told his new hires that he started the company with me and his family. He also told them, "If it wasn't for Brett, we might not be here!" Wow, that made me feel proud! They looked at me and was amazed that I started the company with the owner. After that, the EMS employees were checking out their ambulances for next week, so Akim and I walked away. He was telling me he was trying to get a new contract, so I said, "I hope you get it, Akim!"

"Brett, you have a slow day. I will have Ron and Mark and Scott running the schedule. You have the Russian people you picked up the other day. Take them and bring them back home, and you are done for the day."

I said, "Thank you, Akim."

The year went on. The Ambulance Division was up and running. I had been seeing new employees almost all year, so 2005 came to an end, and 2006 started.

When Akim had his company up and running, he started getting his office together. He placed an ad in the newspaper for a human resource manager, a secretary, and an operations manager. My job was the same since I started with Akim.

After about two weeks, Akim called me and said, "Come to the office." I went to the office, and he introduced me to his new human resource person, secretary, office manager, and operations manager. They were excited to see me because Akim had told them that I started the company with him and his family. He said, "Without, Brett, we might not be here." It made me feel proud! Akim gave me my schedule, which involved some more Russian people, so I ran my schedule, talked to Mark and Ron and Scott, and asked them how their day was going. They said great, so I said, "Have a great day, guys." That day ended too.

A few years went by. The year 2008 came. During that time, as many companies go through, employees came and left. My position didn't change, but what did change was an African American man was running for president of the United States of America. It was exciting for me to see that! I thought I would never see that in my lifetime. We had a bad winter that year. Akim's business was doing good. My life was great. About three months into the year, Akim called me and asked me to meet him at the office, so I went to see what he needed. When I got there, Akim had donuts and coffee. He told me that Scott was quitting the company next week.

I said, "Oh, did he say why?" He said he found another position. "Okay, do you have someone to replace him?" Akim said no. "Brett, do you know anyone?" I said no, right off my head. Akim said he placed another ad in the paper and said he had interviewed some people and looked at the applications that he had received from the ad. He wanted me to tell him if he should hire this couple. I said, "Okay, when can I meet them?"

He said, "They are coming at noon today." I said okay. "Brett, first I need you to go pick up the Russians you picked up last week. You need to pick them up at 10:00 a.m. They should be done at about 11:30 a.m., then drop them off then come back to the office." So I ran the trip and came back to the office.

When I got back, the couple was there with Akim. He introduced them to me. Akim had told them that I started the company with him and his family, so I talked to the couple and asked them if they had any transportation experience. They said they had. I liked them, so I told Akim that they said they had transportation experience. Akim asked, "Brett, do you think they can help our company?"

"I think they can, Akim!"

"Thank you, Brett. I will hire them."

"Okay, Akim." So my title was the driver trainer specialist!

"Brett, we have a slow day. You can take the rest of the day off. Mark and Ron can run the schedule. Tomorrow, I want you to go out with the new hires and train them and see how they do with our clients."

"Okay, I will see you tomorrow," I replied.

The next day, I went to the office. When I got there, Akim had already given them their uniforms. As usual, Akim always had donuts and coffee for his employees. He was a great boss to work for. I showed the new hires how to do the vehicle check, so the new hires and I went out on the road. Their names were Cane and Sara. I liked them, and I told them, "This is a young company, and you guys see how Akim is. He takes care of his employees."

"We see that. We like the company!"

I said, "Just do your job and make plans for your life. You have security here."

"That's good because we just rented an apartment."

"Okay, I will let you guys run the schedule. If you guys need anything from me, just ask me. I'll be sitting here while you guys are running the schedule and picking up the clients and taking them into the facilities and doing the paperwork."

"Okay, Brett."

"Then after you take the client in, call Akim and let him know that you are clear with the trip and see if he wants you to wait on them or have another run for you guys."

"Okay, Brett."

So the day went great! I told Akim the new hires did a good job that day.

"That's good. When do you think they can go out by themselves?"

"Akim, I will go out with them one more day and let them run the schedule with you. After that, they are ready to go out on their own."

"Okay, Brett."

So that day ended.

The next day, I went to the office at about 8:00 a.m., and Akim and the new hires were waiting for me. They greeted me. I said, "Good morning. Are we ready?"

They said, "We are."

I told them, "You guys are going to run the schedule today with Akim. I'm just going to observe how you run operations today."

They said, "Okay, Brett." We went out, and they ran the schedule with Akim. I observed them. The new hires did a great job, and after we got off, I called Akim and told him that they were ready to go out on their own. Akim said, "Okay, Brett, I will let them go out tomorrow."

"Okay, Akim."

"Brett, you can take tomorrow off."

I said, "Thank you, Akim."

That went on for the year. My position was the same as it was when I started. I had the day off the next day, so I got something done around the house. Later that summer of 2008, the country nominated a black candidate for the first time to run for president of the United States of America! It was exciting to see for me as a black man to see an African American man being nominated to run for president of the United States of America! Given the history of black people in America, I never thought I would see this in my lifetime because all my life I had been discriminated! Early in my story, I said I was falsely accused of a crime that I didn't know about. My teacher testified in court that I was in his classroom at the time of the crime, but they still sent me to jail, so that hurt me. I was so disappointed in America as a black man, knowing that this goes on all the time against black people, so I wasn't surprised. I was a juvenile at the time. I was only fourteen years old, and after that, I was sentenced to the Youth Detention Center. Permanently, they sent me over to the country jail, and for the first time ever in my life, I was behind bars. Why did they do that to me? Was it because I committed the crime? Or was it because a Caucasian woman's pocketbook was snatched and it was black guys who snatched her pocketbook? Why did they send me to jail? Was it because I was black? Why did they send me to the country jail and adult jail when I was a juvenile? I was discriminated, and all of my civil rights were violated. It was a shame in America. It was just a shame. Many black people went to jail for nothing and still at this time in history.

CHAPTER 20

I was surprised when America nominated a black man to run for president of the United States. As it got closer to Election Day, November 4, 2008, Americans were divided. They didn't know which way to go. It's never happened before! The election came, November 4. At about nine o'clock that night of the Election Day, America had just elected its first black president, Barack Obama, the first African American and the forty-fourth president of the United States of America.

It was an exciting time in America for black people and white people and all Americans!

The year 2008 came to an end, and a new year was coming in. I had been working for the company for four years now.

The year 2009 came. It was a hard winter that year. It was cold and snowy. Then I began to notice that things were changing in the office. I started to see employees in new uniforms, and I didn't have new uniforms. I was still wearing my old ones. I couldn't understand also. I knew how Akim was. He always let me know what was going on, but now that he was letting his office management run the operations, things were changing for me! I could tell that the office managers, for some reason, didn't like me! I couldn't understand because these were the same employees Akim introduced me to over a year and a half ago. Akim would buy lunch for his employees. The office would ask the employees to come to the office to have lunch that the company had bought, but the new office management never invited me. One day I went to the office when I heard a dispatch asking the employees to come to the office, and that's when I saw them eating pizza. All of the employees were Caucasian, and I was African American. They were the same employees Akim introduced me to when he hired them and told them that I started the company with him and his family. All of a sudden, things started to change for me. I didn't see Mark or the new hires. They were also African Americans, but I did see Ron. He was Caucasian, so I went in and had lunch too because I started the company with the owner. The employees in there were just doing what they were asked to do. I do not think they knew what was going on, so I didn't blame them. I blamed the office management for not letting me know that the company ordered pizza for lunch and they never let me know! That was about the third time I heard this over the radio, so after I had some pizza, I called Akim and let him know what was going on.

He said, "Brett, I will talk to the office managers." I said okay. After that, I could feel more prejudice toward us. It was like they were jealous of us. Mark and I were the only ones who kept the company van at home and the only ones who kept the company computer at home. Mark and I were the only ones who kept the fleet card at home, and Mark and I were the only ones who kept the telephone at home, but we always kept the equipment at home! We didn't ask to keep the equipment at home. The company had trust in us to keep the equipment at home! We had been keeping the equipment at home for four years now. We never thought of it because we always had it from the beginning, and Mark kept his equipment at his home too. We were black and they were white and they didn't like it because black employees seemed to have privilege at the company, but that wasn't true. We earned it. We started the company with Akim and his family.

Mark and I could feel the dislike from the office managers. Akim didn't know this was going on, and the employees were Caucasian, but I noticed that they liked Cane and his friend. They were African American too, but they came in four years after me and Mark started the company. Maybe that's why they liked Cane and his girlfriend because they weren't a threat to them. Well, Mark and I weren't a threat to them either. They were intimidated by us and for no reason!

Mark and I began to feel uncomfortable, so we talked to Akim about this. Akim said he would talk to the office managers and the employees about this. It was like the office managers were trying to make this a racial problem! There was no problem. It's just that we started the company and sought to work together as a team! You shouldn't worry about what other employees have from the company!

That went on, but I didn't have time to worry about that. I was living my life. I started the company with the owner, and I was not going to get caught up in an argument with the office managers, so Mark and I started to ignore them. You could feel the tension. You could cut it with a knife! Mark and I thought it was funny, but we weren't surprised because we had seen it all our life—discrimination!

That went on for the rest of the year! The year 2009 came to an end, and 2010 came in. Just like 2009, there was tension in the office. They were trying to control us. Mark called me and said that he was going to quit because Akim was changing too. I began to notice that too, so about June of 2010, Mark quit! It was just me there. Later that year, after Mark quit, I got written up two times, and then in the winter of 2010, I got suspended! That was an all-time low for me! I couldn't believe that! I didn't believe that Akim authorized them to suspend me when he knew I didn't do anything to deserve that! When I came back off suspension, Akim and I talked about the suspension, and he told me that if I can't get along with the office management, then he can't carry me anymore! I asked Akim, "Why are you doing this to me? Why are you not believing me? Why are you believing the other employees? Don't you know the history of America when it comes to blacks and whites?"

"Brett, yes, I know the history of America. America has just elected its first black president. Brett, Phil is your boss, and you have to listen to him."

I said, "Akim, Phil is the one who lied to you and had you suspend me! So now you believe them over me after everything I did for you and the company! Now you do not believe in me anymore. Thanks, Akim!"

I was very angry! I didn't even want to work at the company anymore. Akim was changing. He believed the other employees over me and believed everything they said about me! I was very disappointed. After all I did for the company, after six years of continuous service and loyalty to the company—and Akim and his family knew my integrity to the company and all the clients liked me—all of a sudden Akim was changing.

During the time I was on suspension, I talked to Mark and told him what was going on, and he said, "Brett, I'm not surprised because I could see it coming. Brett, I know you're still paying on your mortgage, and I am not paying on my mortgage, so I've seen through Akim. After he got the company to where he wanted it, he didn't need me or you, Brett, anymore. That's why I quit, so I'm not surprised, Brett, that Akim is letting the office management take over and letting them discriminate against you! Akim doesn't know it, but they are. Look, Brett, they didn't give you uniforms and never called you to eat lunch that Akim's family provided! They don't let you know what's going on. They don't do anything for you, Brett! Remember when Akim's grandmother passed away, Akim and his family wanted you to drive them to the funeral, but office management didn't let you. They let the new driver Melvin drive the family to the funeral. Akim and his family wanted you to drive them to the funeral. Phil didn't let you. You found out when you called into dispatch for your run, and dispatch told you, 'Brett, you are supposed to be driving the family to the funeral.' Phil, the operations manager, didn't tell you. No, he didn't tell you to go to the funeral and wait on the family."

"Yeah, Mark, I remember, so now, Mark, Akim and his family are letting the office management gang up on me! Akim and his family didn't do anything about that, Mark!"

"What did I tell you, Brett? After all you did for the company this late in the game, they are treating you like his now? Brett, I think they don't need you there anymore! They don't want you there anymore! Brett, I know you don't want to hear this, but I think the office management doesn't want you there, and they are going to try to get you fired!"

"Mark, I think you are right!"

"Brett, watch yourself."

"Okay, Mark, I will let you know what's going on."

"Okay, Brett, have a good day, and don't let them get you down."

That went on for the rest of the year. Akim was indicted on some issues with the state at the time, and he had to go to trial on that. The outcome of Akim going to trial on issues with the state was he was to be removed from the company and was no longer part of it. After I found out the decision of the court, I went out to the house of Akim's mother and told her that I felt threatened by the office management and they're going to fire me! Akim's mother said, "No one can fire you, Brett, but me and my brother, the owners of the company! So, Brett, you don't have to worry."

"Nikita, I'm worried because they already don't like me, and they are trying to get me fired."

"Brett, don't worry. That's not going to happen to you! Brett, you started the company with us. You got us drivers when we needed them. Everyone likes you, and our Russian friends like you too, Brett. You have done a very good job with us, and no one is going to fire you! Don't worry. That's not going to happen to you. Nothing is going to happen!" I hugged her, and she said, "Brett, have a great day."

I said, "Nikita, have a great day too." So 2010 came to an end.

CHAPTER 21

The New Year came in 2011. Akim was no longer with company. His mother was running the company. It was a bad winter that year, but I never missed a day of work. The company ordered new uniforms for the winter, and I started seeing employees with new uniforms, and I didn't get one. I went to the office, and they acted like they didn't have any more uniform, so I just looked in the box and saw the uniforms and took two uniforms. They didn't like it, but at that time, I didn't care! I wasn't going to let them control me or discriminate against me. I knew what Nikita had told me early about my concerns, so I had the strength to do all of that because I started the company with the owner and the office managers were not going to control me! The office managers didn't like it, but I didn't care!

That was the atmosphere at the company!

The operations manager and the human resource manager were a couple. They went together, and the employees couldn't get anything through because the operations manager and the human resource manager were boyfriend and girlfriend. The employees were mad. The company was headed in the wrong direction. The employees were very upset with the company at the time. The company shouldn't have let that happen. There was a lack of interest in the employees because the operations manager and human resource manager were dictating to the employees, and the owner didn't know that they were doing that! I was informing the owner of that, but it was like they didn't care because they let them run the company, and they were turning their employees away! After that, a lot of the employees quit, and the company was going through a bad time because of the operations manager and the human resource manager.

The year went on just like that. Every day I kept seeing new employees and knew that wasn't a good sign. There was a bad attitude at the company. It wasn't the same company I started with! I continued to do my work. It was a bad winter that year, 2011, but it didn't bother me because I was paying my mortgage, and I knew the other employees in the office didn't like me doing so good when I kept seeing them ride by my home, seeing the van parked there. All of the Caucasian employees were jealous of me. Why, I didn't know, but I had an idea because I was an African American. But I started the company with the owner. I will not be intimidated by anyone! That kept happening, but it didn't bother me, so work went on day by day. I had been on salary from day one. I never clocked in, but the rest of the employees had to clock in. The office manager didn't like that! I didn't have to clock in. I could see in their eyes their hatred toward me! I just couldn't understand why, but like I said, it didn't bother me because I saw it all my life—prejudice. With the history of America when it came to Caucasian people and African American people, something will never change! In May of 2011, I got a call from the office. The owner wanted to talk to me that day, so I knew I didn't do anything. *What lie has the office management told them now?* I went to the office, and when I got there, there was a strange atmosphere. I saw the owners. They said, "Hi, Brett." It just seemed strange. The office manager didn't say anything to me, so I knew something was up. I went in the room where the meeting was going to take place. The owners were in the room, and the office manager was in the room. They said, "The reason we wanted you to come to the office is because we have a new time clock system. We know you are on salary, but we need you to start clocking in so we will be able to track your time. Nothing will change for you, Brett, we just need it for tax reasons and if we get audits. If you can start clocking in, that help us keep track of your time."

I said, "That's fine. I will start clocking in tomorrow."

They said, "Thanks, Brett, and this is how it will work every morning. Phil will call you and tell you what time to clock in."

I couldn't understand it. It's like I was a little boy. None of the other employees had to do that! Why me? The office management was getting their way. They were trying to control me now! I could see the smiles on their faces. They were discriminating against me! I had no other choice, so I agreed.

That week, Phil began to call me every morning to let me know when to clock in, so that went on for weeks. One week, Phil called me Monday through Thursday and told me what time to clock in, so I did. That Friday, Phil didn't call me! I called Akim and told him. He said, "Brett, don't worry. You will be all right." I told Akim the agreement was that Phil would call me every morning at 7:00 a.m.

"Brett, maybe he forgot. Go ahead and clock in." So I did. I called Akim's mother and told her what was going on. She said, "Brett, don't worry. I will let Phil know that you clocked in."

I said, "Okay, Nikita," and went on with my day. I had a good day in spite of the things that I was going through and in the way I was feeling. I got off that day. It was the weekend. That weekend, they had some festivals going on like the Ribs and Blues and Summer Festivals, which were coming up that weekend. I was looking forward to the upcoming festivals, so I had a great weekend at the Ribs and Blues Festival. The workweek came up. I was looking forward to having a great day at work that week. I loved my job. The people I met were great. I enjoyed my job, so I had a great day at work. When I dropped off my last run for the day, the office called me and said, "We need you to come to the office." I wondered, *For what?* I went to the office to see what the office needed. When I went into the office, everyone was waiting for me, as if I did something. They said, "Hi, Brett, the meeting is going to be in this room." I went into the room where the meeting was going to be, and the operations manager and the human resource manager were in the room and said, "Brett, we are firing you because you clocked in and Phil didn't tell you to clock in."

I said, "Phil didn't call me, so I called Akim and let him know that Phil didn't call me. Akim said, 'Don't worry, Brett, I will let Phil know you clocked in, and I called Akim's mother to let her know."

They said, "We don't care. You were not to clock in until Phil called you."

"Lynn, the agreement was that Phil was to call me at seven o'clock every morning. He called me that week, but he didn't call me on Friday."

They said, "You shouldn't have clocked in, Brett. You are fire! At that time, Akim's mother looked into the room and looked at me and didn't say anything. They took my keys to the van and all the equipment that I had, the cell phone, computer, fleet card, etc. The owner gave them to me when I first started with the company. I couldn't believe it! They escorted me off the property, and Phil drove me home.

It was unbelievable what just happened to me. After all these years of total dedication and loyalty to the company and representing the company to its finest, they fired me! Just like that, as if I didn't mean anything to the company. It wasn't right, and it wasn't fair!

After Phil dropped me off at my home, I could see that he took great delight in that. I was thinking, *I'm going to lose my home and everything I work for.* I went into my house and sat down. I was in shock! But I didn't let that mess up my day, knowing that they fired me for nothing!

I didn't call anyone. I just sat in my house for a long time, quiet, and was thinking a lot about everything I just went through, working for a company that I loved and enjoyed, and now I was unemployed!

When the next day came, I didn't go out the door. That was unusual for me because ever since I started the job, every day I went outside my door, except on weekends. I went to work happy and looking forward to each day. Now I was just at home with a mortgage and no way to pay it! I won't lie. I was concerned that I might lose my home. I know they fired me for nothing. I know they really wanted to do that! The owners whom I trusted and worked for and had been in their homes didn't believe me. They didn't seem to care how I suffered because of their lies.

I called a lady. Her name was Mrs. Kelly. I told her I needed to talk to her, so she invited me out to her house. Mrs. Kelly was the lady I met in 1994 after my wife left me. She was a volunteer tax preparation assistant for a program to help low-income people. I met Mrs. Kelly at the library, and she prepared my taxes for me. She told me that she would in the years to come help me with my taxes. I appreciated that! Mrs. Kelly took a liking to me! She still prepared my taxes each year from 1994 to 2016, and she knew the company I was working for because she had done my taxes for that company. I got to Mrs. Kelly's house. She was happy to see me, and I was happy to see her because she was like a mother to me! Mrs.

Kelly helped me with a lot of things like a mother would for her son! We sat down. I could see that she was wondering what was on my mind, and I told her that the company I started with just fired me for nothing. She was surprised and shocked! She asked me, "Brett, why did they fire you?"

I told Mrs. Kelly, "They have a new time clock system, and they needed me to start clocking in for tax reasons and if they get an audit. They said, 'This is how it will work: Phil will call you every morning at seven and tell you what time to clock in.' So he did that for a couple of weeks. One Friday, he didn't call me, so I called Akim, the man I started the company with, and told him that Phil didn't call me. Akim said, 'Brett, don't worry. I will let Phil know. You clock in.' I said okay and hung up. Then I called Akim's mother and told her the same thing, and she said, 'Don't worry, Brett, I will tell Phil that you called me and told me what was going on and I told you to clock in.' We hung up. That's why they fired me because I clocked in without Phil's permission!"

Mrs. Kelly couldn't believe it. I could see that she was concerned about me. I could see that she was wondering, *Brett, how will you pay your mortgage?* I could see that she can see that I was scared, alone, and hurt. I was, and I started to cry, and she hugged me. I needed her. I needed my mother. She was never there for me! Mrs. Kelly was there for me, so she kept looking at me. She was a Caucasian lady, and she really cared about me.

No matter what I had been through in my life, I will always know that there are good and bad people in America. Even back in the days of slavery, there were good and bad people, like the Quakers—they were good people! They didn't want to see their country built on the backs of African slaves!

After my meeting with Mrs. Kelly was over, she said, "Brett, you are a good man. After all these years, I can't see you doing anything wrong! Brett, keep your head up. You will find another job. You are a good man." She hugged me again, and I left and went home.

The next day, I called Mark and let him know what the company had done to me. "Mark, they fired me."

"They fired you? Brett, why did they fire you? For what?"

"One day the office called me and said the owner wanted to talk to me, so I went to the office to see what they needed. When I got there, the office management said the meeting will be in a certain room, so I went into the room, and Phil and Lynn were in there and said, 'We want you to start clocking in. We know you are on salary, but we need you to start clocking in so we can keep track of your time for tax reasons and in case we get audited.' I said okay. 'Brett, this is how it's going to work: Phil will call you every morning at seven and let you know what time to clock in,' so I said okay. 'Brett, that starts tomorrow, okay?' So Phil started to call me to tell me my start time. That went on for weeks. One Friday, Phil didn't call me, so I called Akim and told him. Akim said, 'Clock in, Brett, I will tell Phil.' I called Akim's mother and told her, and she said, 'Brett, don't worry. I will tell Phil I told you to clock in because he didn't call you.' Mark, I went into work that Monday. When I got off that day, the office called me to come to the office. When I got to the office, I saw Phil and Lynn in the office. They said, 'You are fired!' I asked, 'For what?' 'You clocked in, and Phil didn't tell you to clock in!' 'Phil didn't call me. I called Akim and his mother, and they told me to clock in because Phil didn't call and they will tell Phil that.' 'We don't care. You are fired!'"

Mark said, "Come on, Brett, they did that?"

"That's what they did."

"Brett, after all you've done for Akim and his family, they fired you like that! See, that's not right, Brett, that's why I quit. I could see what the company was coming to! When Akim was indicted, I could see that the company was in trouble, and all the office managers they hired didn't like me and you, Brett. Remember when the company ordered new uniforms? They never told us, did they, Brett?"

"You are right, Mark."

"They never told us to come to the office to have pizza that the company bought. All of the other employees were eating lunch. They told them, didn't they?"

"You're right, Mark."

"Remember, Brett, when Akim's grandmother passed away, the family wanted you to drive them to the funeral, but Phil didn't let you, did he?"

"You're right, Mark, he let the new employee transport the family to the funeral."

"Brett, you only found out when you called dispatch to get a run for the day, and dispatch told you, 'Brett, you're supposed to be transporting the family to the funeral.' Phil didn't tell you, 'Brett, go to the funeral. Call us. We will give you directions.'"

"You see, Brett, me and you saw them all come in, and look at them now! Akim's family let them fire you after all you did for the company! Brett, Akim's not there anymore, and the family let the office management run all over you! And the family let them fire you! Unbelievable, Brett, look at all the drivers you got for them."

"I know, Mark, unbelievable."

"Brett, I know you're not in a position to fight them because you have a mortgage payment. They know you have a mortgage payment. After all you've done for them, they let the office management discriminate you! Brett, I'm sorry to hear this now. I'm mad!"

"Mark, I'm going to call Akim's mother to ask why she let them fire me, and I will let you know what I find out."

"Okay, Brett, don't let it get you down!"

"Thanks, Mark. Talk to you later."

"Bye. Oh, before I forget, I saw a Caucasian man driving my van. It was Phil and Lynn's friend. A driver called me to let me know, and the driver told me no one liked Phil and Lynn for what they did to you, Brett! They said, 'We all believe you, and we are mad about it!'"

"Thanks. I needed to hear that. Tell them I will be back!"

CHAPTER 22

Wednesday of that week, I called Akim's mother and explained to her I didn't do anything. I asked her, "Why did you let them fire me when I told you that was going to happen, and they fired me! You told me, 'Brett, no one can fire you but me and my brother,' so you and your brother let them fire me, so y'all gave them permission to fire me, Nikita?" That wasn't right. She didn't have anything to say because she knew it was true!

Nikita said she would call me later that week. I said okay, so later that week, she called and said, "Brett, I'm going to get you back on with us because I know you did everything right!"

I said, "Nikita, you should never let them fire me anyway!" She didn't say anything. I said, "Nikita, you know I have a mortgage to pay. Why would I do something that stupid? You know that I was loyal to the company. You know that. You have been to my home. You and Akim let me keep the van and the phone, the computer, and the fleet card at home! The trust the company had in me, why would I throw all of that away? Nikita, ask yourself, 'Why would Brett do something like that?' The agreement was that Phil would call me every morning at seven and tell me what time to clock in. He was doing that, but that Friday of that week, he didn't call me!

"I called you and Akim and told you what was going you, and Akim said, 'Brett, don't worry. We will let Phil know. For whatever reason he didn't call, we told you, Brett, to clock in.' I had a great Friday, got off, and had a great weekend. I came to work on Monday and had a great day at work, and when I got off, I was asked to come to the office where they fired me! Nikita, you looked in the room and said nothing to me! Nikita, I was hurt that you didn't say anything to me! Now I'm at home with no job, no money!" She didn't say anything because she knew that I had told her over a year ago that this was going to happen. She couldn't say anything, then she finally said something. "Brett, I'm going to get you back here where you belong!"

"Nikita, I have no money. I don't have anything. This is really tough for me that you're actually letting them fire me!"

She said, "I will get you back!"

I said, "Okay, when will that happen?" She said soon. "Nikita, I have no money."

"Brett, I will give you some money. I will call you tomorrow and tell you where to meet me, okay?"

I said, "Thanks, Nikita," and we hung up.

The next day, she called me and told me where to meet her, so I did. She showed up. I got out of my car and hugged her. I was glad to see her. She had a big smile on her face, and she said, "Brett, I want you to call Phil and leave him a message and tell him that he's the operations manager and he's your boss." So I did. Nikita was looking at me. After that, we got into her car, and she gave some money. I was happy because I needed it. She was telling me, "I will get you back."

I said, "I need my job."

She said, "I know." I hugged her, and she said, "Brett, have a good day. I will be talking to you soon." I said okay and got out of her car, and I left.

I went back home feeling good about the conversation we had, and I was encouraged that Nikita was going do everything she could to get me back. I believed her, so I had a pretty good day in spite of everything I'd been through. I had time on my hands, so I did some things around the house. The next day came, and it had been two weeks since I'd been fired. I needed to get back to work because I needed to make money. This was very unusual for me. This was heartbreaking! I didn't hear from Nikita that day, and I didn't call her. I just sat around the house and thought about the day I started to work at the company. I started the company with them. I was missing all the places and facilities I went to. I loved it and should not be at home! That day came to an end. The next day, at about 9:00 a.m., I was sitting at home drinking my coffee when the telephone rang. I answered it, and it was Nikita on the other end. She said, "Brett, you can start back to work on Monday of next week!" I was so happy to be going back to work. Nikita said, "Brett, I will see you next week. Your start time will be at 7:00 a.m."

I said, "Thank you, Nikita, for believing in me! I look forward to coming back to work and doing the job I did when I first started with the company! Thank you very much for all you have done!"

That same day, I called Mrs. Kelly and told her the company hired me back. She was surprised! I told her, "I'm still upset over it, but I will still do a great job for the company."

She said, "Brett, that's great! What an attitude, to take after what they did to you!"

I said, "I will talk to you later, Mrs. Kelly."

"Brett, keep your head up. You will get past this!" I needed the encouraging words, so I told Mrs. Kelly, "I would let you know how things are going!"

She said, "I'm glad you are back to work."

"Thank you." We then hung up.

That same day, I called Mark and told him that they hired me back. "What? Brett, they hired you back? Can you believe it? See, Brett, their conscience got to them. They knew they fired you for nothing."

"Unbelievable, Mark. I will call you back when I see how things are going now that I'm back."

"Okay, Brett, be careful."

"I will. Okay, bye, Mark."

So next week came, and I went back to work. The employees were glad to see me back. They said, "We never believe what Phil and Lynn said about you! You are the one that started this company, that's why we all have a job!"

I said, "Thank you, guys. I'm glad to be back." I talked to the employees for a while, then I got into the van and got dispatch for my run. It was great being back, but I was still hurt! I could tell that the employees felt bad that I had to go through what they put me through. I had a good day back. I didn't see Phil or Lynn, but I knew they knew I was back, so that day ended. I couldn't take the van home, but that was okay.

The next day, I went to work. When I got to the station, I saw Phil. He looked like he was mad, but you know what, I didn't care! I wasn't intimated by him, and I got into my van and went to work. I had a great day. There were no problems that day, just another day at work doing the same thing I was doing when I started the company with the owner! It was just like old times, you know, just did my job. I thought about what I was doing in my life, paying my mortgage and my bills, so that week ended. I didn't hear anything from Phil or Lynn, so they must have been told not to bother me, to leave me alone. The owners must have told them, "We like Brett. He is a big part of our company! He's a part of our team, so don't bother him." That was my thinking.

I was never intimidated, and I would not be intimidated. I'm a hard worker. Months went by. I had relaxed. I had put the issue behind me. I was thinking about my future and what I was doing in my life. I was no longer thinking about what they might try to do to me because Nikita had already addressed that issue. I was doing my job, and things were fine. In June of 2012, I got a call from Nikita. She told me, "Phil is going to call you and tell you that you can start taking the van back home." That was great news. Things were being restored back to me, which they should have been done when I first got back, but I was not complaining. I was just glad that things were coming back to me the way they were when I started getting the respect from the owner that I deserved!

The year 2012 came to an end. It was a great year for me. I was looking forward to 2013.

CHAPTER 23

The year 2013 came. The company was growing. Phil was Phil, but I wasn't intimidated by him or Lynn! I did my job, and I kept on thinking about what I was doing in my life. Months went by. It was a bad winter in 2013. Spring came. It felt good to be out of winter. All the ice and snow was melting. I was looking forward to warmer temperature and plants and flowers growing, so now that spring was here, I would be putting down some fertilizer to get my lawn back green again. Work was going good, but I knew that anything that someone said about me, they would believe it whether true or false! It was still like I was walking on pins and needles, but I was fine with that because I knew that the owner was behind me.

Spring had come and gone. Going in to the month of June, summer will be here soon—time for mosquitoes, flies, insects, etc.

Work was going good. I was looking forward to a great summer, getting out of the house, walking more. I will be paying off my home in three years. I can't wait till that time comes. I had been in my home for twenty-three years. I was on the biweekly plan that saved me six years on my thirty-year mortgage, so it'd been a long journey, and it'd been a great experience! I had a great job that I loved to work and come to every day. Everything looked good, so I was going into the summer of 2013 with a good outlook!

A week and half into June, I was dispatched to a nursing facility to transport a lady to her medical appointments, so I transported her to her appointment and waited for her so I could take her back to the facility, and I did. That was my last run for the day, so dispatch called me and asked me to come to the office. I was wondering what they wanted with me. I knew I hadn't done anything, so I went to the office. The office manager said, "The lady client said that you kissed her on her lips." I said I didn't, and the office manager said, "Brett, we have to let you go!"

"For what?"

"Our client said you kissed her on the lips. Brett, you are fired! We will do an investigation to see if the allegation is true. Meanwhile, we have to fire you, Brett!"

"Why? I didn't do anything."

"Because our client said you kissed her, we have to fire you. Do you have a way home? No? Then Phil will take you home." The office manager said, "We will do an investigation and let you know what happens."

"If you are going to do an investigation, why do you have to fire me? Why not just suspend me without pay? The investigation should only take no more than two weeks."

"Brett, we have to fire you! That's all we are going to say! This meeting is over. Phil, would you take Brett home." Phil took me home. Three weeks passed, and no word from the office. I think they lied to me about an investigation. No one called me to let me know what was going on with the investigation, so I called the office. No one would talk to me about the investigation. It was like they were covering something up, so I was fired and unemployed.

I called a friend, Awal, who had a transportation company. The name of his company was Health Ride, and I told him what just happened to me. He said, "Brett, you started the company with them. Why would they do that to you?"

"The office management was biased toward me! They didn't like me, and they were just waiting on someone to accuse me of anything so they could fire me, whether it was true or not! They didn't care, and the owner was behind them, so I didn't have a chance."

My friend said, "Well, Brett, I can't believe they did that to you! Brett, I have a position for you! I have a van in the shop. It's going to take a week or two, but once it gets out, you will have a job again, and you will work for us."

"Thank you a lot. I really appreciate it, Awal."

He got the van out of the shop, and I went to work with the new company.

It was great to be back at work, meeting new people and new clients. The new company was different. It was a little slower, but I loved it. The boss was easy to work with. I had to work six days a week, but it was better than not working at all. Months went by. Going into the holidays, winter was coming. By this time, I was secure in my job. I knew the routine and the schedule, and I knew the clients and the facilities to take them to, so I was very comfortable.

Thanksgiving came. I spent a quiet holiday at home by myself. I did bake turkey breasts and make some dressing and sweet potatoes and some green beans and mashed potatoes. I just enjoyed the holiday, and I was just very thankful that I was back at work and paying my mortgage. I have to say going into December was a lot of stress. Five months had passed since I was fired, but I was glad that the year was ending.

I have to say that being fired was stressing me out, but I was glad to be working with the new company. What just happened to me was unbelievable. I couldn't believe it! It was unfair! After everything I'd done for the company, they fired me twice—this time for good! They knew I had a mortgage! They knew that I was an excellent employee, yet they did it because they wanted to do it because they didn't need me anymore. I was still trying to get over that. Otherwise, things were going good for me. I was getting ready for Christmas.

Two weeks into December, I was transporting some clients to their appointment, and I wasn't feeling good. I dropped them off at their appointment and waited on them, but I just wasn't feeling good! They came out of their appointment, and I loaded them back into the van and started to transport them back home. That's when I started to get really dizzy. There was a nurse aide with the client. She could see something wasn't right, so I stopped the van in the middle of the street, and I asked the nurse if the van was spinning in the middle of the street. She said, "No, Brett." That's when I knew I was in trouble. The nurse said, "Brett, I think your blood sugar is low." I didn't know if the stress of everything I'd been through was catching up with me, but something wasn't right! I didn't know what it was. I just thought that I was tired and I just wasn't feeling good. I still wasn't feeling good, so I called my boss and told him that I wasn't feeling good and asked him if I could take the rest of the day off. He said, "We are slow today, Brett. Take the day off, and call me later and let me know if you can work tomorrow." I said okay. That day was Friday the 13ᵗʰ, so we had work on Saturday. I did call my boss back later that day and told him that I still wasn't feeling good. He said, "Take the weekend off and call me Sunday to let me know if you can work Monday of next week." I said okay. I got a good night's sleep Friday night. I woke up Saturday feeling good. I wasn't feeling bad like I was feeling on Friday. I felt like myself again, so I had a great day off. I called my boss and told him that I could work next week, and he said, "Brett, that's great, because we picked up some new clients, and we're going to be a little busy next week. How are you feeling, Brett?"

"I'm feeling a lot better that good, Awal. I'll see you next week. Have a great day."

"Okay, Brett, you too. I will call you Monday about 7:00 a.m. and let you know your first pickup."

"Okay, thank you. Bye."

When I went to bed Saturday night, I got a good night's sleep. When I woke up Sunday morning, the whole side of my face was numb. I knew I was having a stroke! I called the company that just fired me because they were an EMS, and then I told them, "I think I'm having a stroke. I need an ambulance." They sent an ambulance, but they didn't send their ambulance. They sent Clayton Medical EMS. I couldn't get out of the bed. I tried to get up, but I was dizzy. I was feeling like I wanted to throw up. When I looked at the bedroom door, it seemed like a hundred or so doors. I knew I was having a stroke and I was in an emergency!

I heard someone knocking at the door, but I couldn't get out of my bed, so I just rolled out of my bed and sat on my buttocks and pushed myself toward the stairs. When I got to the stairs, I pushed myself on my buttocks all the way down the stairs, and I crawled to my back door. I opened the door, and there was a policeman and the emergency ambulance out there.

They were trying to get into the house, and then once I opened the door, I fell out. They asked me what was going on. I said, "I think I am having a stroke." They took me to the hospital.

Once we got to the ER, they took me inside, and it's like they were waiting for me, and they were ready for me. They hooked me up to a machine, and I started getting really dizzy. I was having a migraine. I started throwing up. I thought I was dying. I remember them putting me in a big machine, and then I passed out. I can't remember anything after that.

I woke up a day or two later in the ICU. When I opened my eyes, I saw doctors standing around me, and they were writing on pads. I stayed in the ICU for a couple of days, and then they took me to the brain and stroke floor where I stayed until they discharged me.

Later in December, they discharged me from the hospital, and my boss came and transported me home. I thanked him, and he said, "Brett, when your doctor clears you, come back to work. You still have a job!"

I said, "Thank you, Awal."

He left, and I went into my house. It was great to be back at home. The only thing I could do was turn on the heat and get in the bed!

I stayed in bed all night and got a good night's sleep. The next morning, I felt like I felt when I was in the hospital. The hospital took good care of me. They saved my life! I was very grateful for the hospital taking such good care of me! I am now a stroke survivor!

I stayed in bed and couldn't get up. I needed help, so I called a friend and told her that I had a stroke. She said, "What?"

I said, "I had a stroke."

"Why didn't you call me?"

I told her that I was fighting for my life. I couldn't help myself. I was incapacitated. She said, "Oh, I wasn't thinking. How are you recovering from your stroke, Brett?"

"It isn't fun. I could have died, but I didn't. Other than that, I feel okay. The hospital took good care of me."

She said, "Brett, that's great! How can I help you?"

I said, "I need something to eat. I can't get out of the bed, and I can't get up to cook me something to eat."

She said, "What do you have a taste for?"

"Something simple, like some chicken noodle soup. I need something to warm me up."

She said, "Brett, I will bring some soup up to you."

"Thank you."

Later that morning, Barbara called me and said she was on her way up to me. I said, "Call me when you get to the back door." She said okay, and we hung up. About a half hour passed, and the phone started to ring. I picked it up, and she said, "I'm in the back." I told her, "Give me a moment, and I will be right down." I went downstairs to let her in. I was glad to see her. She was the first person I saw since I got out of the hospital. She was glad to see me. She brought the soups over, and she opened me a couple of cans of chicken noodle soup, and I ate them. The soup was good for me, full of nourishment. She brought some stew too, and some greens. We talked a little, and she said, "Brett, I can see you had a stroke. I want you to get back in bed and stay there."

I said, "I will because it's going to be a long time before I'm back on my feet."

She said, "Call me if you need something." I said okay, and she left.

I went back upstairs and got back in bed and watched TV.

I was thinking about my mortgage. I was discharged in late December of 2013, but I did pay my December mortgage payment!

Before I had a stroke, I saw on TV a program for people who needed help with their mortgage. I wrote that telephone number down, not thinking that I would ever need it or that I would have a stroke, but I did write it down, and I kept it!

CHAPTER 24

The next day, I called the number. A lady picked up and said, "Thanks for calling Save the House. How can I help you?"

I said, "My name is Brett Jones, and I had a stroke two weeks ago."

"Wow, how are you?"

"I'm doing the best I can right now."

She said, "Great! How can we help you?"

"I saw an ad on TV saying that you can help me with my mortgage if I had lost my job by outsourcing or I had a medical emergency and could no longer work or pay my mortgage."

She said, "Our program is called Save the House, and it's for people just like you, Brett, someone who had a medical emergency or someone whose job was outsourced to another country." I told her what I was going through, and she said, "Brett, we do not do applications over the phone, but you can pick up an application at our office. I told her, "I can't get out of bed, and I have no one that can come up to the office to pick up an application." She put me on hold for a moment, and she said, "Brett, let me go speak to my supervisor and see if we can do a special help for you because you had a stroke and I know it's hard for you right now. Just one moment." I was on hold for a moment, and she came back to the phone and said, "Brett, my supervisor said we can do your application over the phone." I was so happy. She did the application over the phone. "Brett, you are a good candidate for our program." It was an exciting news for me!

The lady said, "It's going to take about thirty days for us to process your application. We will be in touch with you."

I said, "Thank you very much." We hung up.

All day I was thinking about the lady who helped me with my application. She gave me hope.

A week went by, and New Year was coming in 2014. I was feeling a little better. I knew it was going to take some time for me to recover from my stroke, but I was in good spirits. So 2014 came in. It was a New Year, but I knew that I needed help. It was a new world for me now! I needed help in getting assistance, so I called a friend, Risa, in Chicago, and I told her that I had a stroke and I needed her to come down and help me to get assistance.

She said, "I would be glad to come down to help you, Brett!" I told her that I would pay for her round-trip bus ticket. She said, "I will call the bus station and see what's the best and fastest ticket I can get, and I will call you and tell you when I can come down." I said thank you. A day later, she called and said, "Brett, I bought the tickets, and I will be down in two days."

I said, "Thank you, and I will see you when you get here." The day was Wednesday, and she got to my place on Friday at 10:00 a.m. She called me and said, "I'm here, and I will see you soon, Brett." She had her friend come and pick her up from the bus station.

Risa got to my place. I was downstairs waiting for her and her friend, and then they pulled up. Her friend helped her with her suitcases, and they brought them into the house. Risa introduced me to her friend, and I thanked her friend for bringing Risa to my house. Her friend left, and I took Risa to one of my guest rooms. She said, "Brett, I like this guest room."

I said, "Thank you, Risa." She got settled in, and then she came in the next room where I was, and we began to talk. She was asking me how I felt after my stroke. I told her that I was feeling a little better, but it's going to take a long time for me to recover from my stroke. It's getting later in the evening, and she said, "Brett, are you getting hungry?"

I said, "Risa, there's some beef stew downstairs. You can warm up. It's enough for both of us. There's some ham and cheese and other stuff down there. You can look in the fridge and see what's in there." She said okay, so she warmed up the beef stew, and she made herself a ham and cheese sandwich. We ate dinner, and we talked a little more. She said, "Brett, we will go down to the service center on Monday to get you the assistance you need. I know you've never done this before, but I know how it works. You will need these documents to take down there: your social number, your birth certificate, you need your mortgage statement, you need your last check stub from last year, and your tax returns from last year."

"Risa, I have all of them. I anticipated that, so I have them all ready for you right here." We looked them over, and she said, "Oh, Brett, that's great." We put them in a folder, and she said, "Brett, I'm going to let you get some rest." I said, "Thank you, Risa," and she went back to her room, and I lay down and went to sleep.

The next day, Saturday morning, Risa made some coffee, and she fixed me some cereal. She had some bacon and eggs and hash browns. It'd been about three weeks since I was discharged from the hospital. I was feeling a little stronger, but I knew it's going to take a long time to recover. We finished our breakfast, and Risa washed the dishes up while I went back to my bedroom and lay down. After Risa cleaned up, she came back upstairs, and she went into her room and called Chicago to let them know how things were going. Later that day, Risa fixed dinner. We ate, and then we watched some TV together. Then I went to bed, so did she.

Sunday came. Risa got up and fixed breakfast and coffee. We ate and drunk some coffee. She cleaned up, and she said, "Brett, I wanted to look over the documents you have because we really want to make sure that we have everything so when we get down there, we don't have to come back there because we forgot to bring a document." We looked them over, and she said, "I think we got everything covered, Brett. We want to be up at 5:30 a.m. to be there at 7:00 a.m. because there's going to be a line."

I said, "Okay, Risa." She went back to her room and talked to Chicago and her friends, and then she lay down and rested a little. Later that day, Risa fixed dinner. She fried some chicken, and she made some green beans with potatoes and some macaroni and cheese, and I had some dinner rolls, which she also made. We had a really good dinner! That was the first solid dinner I had since I was discharged from the hospital, so I was getting stronger.

When Monday came, we both were up about 5:30 a.m. and getting ready to go to the service center. I had never been there before, but I needed help, so we got there around 7:00 a.m. She was right. There was a line, so we stood in line, and the building opened at 7:30 a.m. We went in, took a ticket, and sat down and waited till my number was called. When my number was called, we went to the desk, and the lady asked, "Can I help you?"

Risa said, "My friend had a stroke, and we are down here for help to get him assistance for food, medical, and cash."

The lady said, "We can help him with that." The lady gave us an application and said, "Take it upstairs to the second floor and fill it out, and someone will call you in for an interview." We filled out the application and waited awhile, then a lady called my name, and we went in for my interview. The lady was very nice. She asked me some questions about income. "Brett, do you have any money coming in?" I said no. She asked me, "Is anyone living with you, Brett?" I said no, so the lady was putting the information that I had given her into her computer. Risa and I sat there and waited for her to finish her work, and she did. She said, "Mr. Jones, you qualify for food and medical assistance."

I said, "Thank you! This is good news!" She smiled like she wanted to help me, and then she said, "You can go on our website and check your progress with your ID number. Put your ID number in the category box, and it will bring up your case and tell you when your benefits will start."

"Thank you."

She said, "Mr. Jones, your interview is over. Good luck and get better!"

I said, "Thank you!"

Risa and I left the lady's office. I was so relieved. I felt so good because I didn't have anything, no money, no food, nothing! We were down there for about four hours or so, but it was worth every minute of it!

Risa and I left and went back home. She was saying, "Now we have to get you CCDI, so when we get back to the house, we are going to call CC and get an application so you can get on the CC Disability Insurance." We got home, and she called CC, and she gave them my information. They asked to speak to me, so Risa gave me the phone. I said hello, and the lady said, "Hi, Brett." I said hi. She said, "We have an appointment date for you. It's going to be February 15, 2014, by phone." I said thank you, and she asked me if I had any questions for her. I said, "No, ma'am, not at this time."

I really appreciated that. I was looking forward to my interview for disability.

Risa was happy for me. I was happy as well. All that week I was showing her what I had been doing, like how I filled out an application for housing assistance. She asked, "How is that going?"

"Good. I should hear something in about thirty days."

She said, "Good. I hope you qualify for the program."

"Thank you."

It was the first week of the New Year, January. It was Thursday of that week, and Risa was telling me that she was going to have her friend come and pick her up so she can spend some time with her nephews. I said, "That's great, Risa. I will be okay."

"Are you sure?"

"I will be okay."

Her friend came over later that day. Risa introduced us to each other. I said, "Have a great time." They said okay. Risa said, "If you need me, call me." I said okay, and they left.

I was feeling good about the week I had, going down to the service center, being approved for benefits, food stamps, medical, and filling out an application over the phone for an appointment date for CC, so I was having a great week.

I relaxed while Risa was gone. She called me on Friday and asked how I was doing. I said okay. She said, "I will see you tomorrow about 4:00 p.m."

"Okay. see you then."

I had a good night's sleep Friday, and Saturday morning came. I fixed myself some coffee and relaxed a little and was thinking about what I just went through. It was unbelievable!

Risa came back about 5:00 p.m. Saturday. I had dinner all ready for her. We ate, and she was glad to see her nephews. I said, "That's great, Risa." On Sunday, Risa was going back to Chicago. She had been with me for a week, and what a week it was!

Sunday came. I thanked Risa for all her help, and she said, "Brett, I was glad to help you!" I said thank you. It was about noon Sunday, and Risa said, "My bus leaves at 3:00 p.m., and my friend is on her way over to get me so I could see the kids before I leave."

I said, Thank you, Risa, for everything you've done for me."

"You're welcome, Brett." Her friend pulled up. Risa gave me a hug and said, "I will call you when I get back to Chicago."

"Have a safe trip."

"I will." Then she left.

I felt good that I was going to start getting assistance. I was still worried about my mortgage, and I was still worried about what CC's decision would be.

I had some savings that I was living off, but I knew that it would only last me a couple of months. While we were down at the service center, the lady told me about a program called Care. "This program will help you with your utilities. You need to go down to 700 Crown Road and fill out an application." That next week, I went down to Care and filled out an application and took all the documents they needed. After filling out the application, the lady said, "Mr. Jones, we have an intake lady that will be seeing you soon, so stay here, and someone would call your name." I sat there, and about twenty minutes later, a lady called my name, and she interviewed me and said, "Mr. Jones, you qualify for our program. Your monthly gas and electric bills will be ten dollars a month. Make sure you pay your bills each month because at the end of the year, you will get a credit. If you don't pay your bills, you will have to pay the full bill, so pay your bills each month on time, Brett!"

"I will."

"We will send you a letter out when you have to apply again."

I said, "Thank you and have a nice day."

"You too, Mr. Jones." I left.

I went back home, and things were starting to come together. *I will be getting assistance with food and with medical now. I'm also on Care now! This is great.* I took it one day at a time. February was coming up. February 15 was the day that I would be doing my interview over the phone for CC., and I was thinking about that. I was kind of nervous, but at the same time I had a stroke. I'm a stroke survivor. I was talking to the lady at CC who was setting up my interview. She said, "Mr. Jones, you've been putting in to CC forty-two years, and I don't see a problem with you being approved for CC. That's what it was set up for. It's for people like you, Mr. Jones, people who had a medical emergency, and that's what the program is." That was reassuring, or so I had hoped going into my interview.

The day of my interview came, February 15. My appointment time was 10:00 a.m. It was 8:00 a.m., and I was nervous, but I was confident. So 10:00 a.m. came, and I didn't hear the phone ring. I sat by the phone and waited. About 10:09, the phone rang, and I picked up. It was the CC lady. She said, "Can I speak to Brett Jones?" I said, "This is him."

"My name is Sharon, and I will be doing your interview." I said I was a little nervous, but I was ready.

She said, "That's good." The lady conducted the interview. It took about twenty-two minutes. The interview was mostly about my financial. When the interview was over, the representative said, "Mr. Jones, CC will be in touch with you in about sixty to ninety days from this date."

"Okay, Mrs. Sharon."

She asked me, "Mr. Jones, do you have any questions for me?" I said no. Mrs. Sharon said, "Get better, Mr. Jones." I said thank you, and we hung up.

I was glad the interview was over. I had done everything that I had to do to get assistance. Now I was still thinking about my mortgage and hoping that I would be approved for the program.

CHAPTER 25

A couple of months went by. I was running out of savings, so I called my previous employer and asked him if he could help me until I get my CC, and he said he would. Awal said, "Brett, I will give you a hundred dollars a month for four months. "Thank you, Awal," I said. He did that. It helped me out a lot! I called another friend who I thought was a friend, but it seemed like when I had a medical emergency, I couldn't get in touch with her. At the time, I couldn't understand. Eventually I did get in touch with two friends. I asked one if I could borrow fifty dollars, and her voice changed all of a sudden. She didn't sound like the friend I knew before my stroke. She hesitated a little and said, "Brett, I will get back to you on that." I was surprised, but I said thank you, and we hung up.

I wasn't feeling good about the conversation I just had with a friend, but that's all I had.

I called another friend and asked her if she can help me with twenty dollars a month till I get my CC. She said she would help me. I said, "Thank you, IyanIa."

She said, "Brett, when will you need it?"

"Starting next month." She said okay, but I never heard from her again.

The other friend called me. Her name was Barbara. She said, "Brett, I can let you borrow thirty dollars." I said, "Thank you. That will help me!"

She asked, "Brett, when can you pay it back?"

"Barbara, I will pay you back when I get my CC. The lady said it would take up two sixty days or ninety days." It didn't sound like she liked that, but she said okay, and we hung up. After talking to her, I didn't want to take the money from her. I never had to ask anyone for money, but you never know when you might need a friend in an emergency, so I took the money.

April came, and my mortgage company was understanding of my situation, and they helped me as much as they could, but they had a process they had to go through before going into foreclosure. They did everything to help me!

May of 2014 came, and I received a letter from an attorney's firm. The letter stated that my mortgage company had ordered them to start foreclosure on the property at Pine Street.

All of a sudden, I got scared and nervous, and I was all alone. There was nothing I could do at the time. I had an interview coming up with St. Ruth Health for a poster board for stroke survivors. The day came to do the interview. Before I received the letter from the attorney's firm. I was excited for this interview! I was looking very much forward to it. When the day came to take the interview, the phone rang. I picked up, and a lady said, "Can I speak with Brett Jones." I said, "I'm him."

"Good morning. My name is Laura. I'm going to interview you for the poster board." I have to say I was nervous, so she started the interview, but I couldn't concentrate because I was thinking about the letter I just got from the attorney's office. She listened to me and felt for me, and I told her, "I'm sorry for telling you about my worries."

She said, "Brett, I understand. It is not easy to recover financially from a medical emergency. You are a stroke survivor, so I understand your concerns and your fears, so this is okay, Brett." We ended the interview, and she said, "Brett, you will be all right." I was scared, and I was alone, but she reassured me that I would be okay. She gave me hope! I thanked her, and she said, "Brett, have a great day." I said thank you, and we hung up.

May ended, and June came in, and I had been thinking about selling one of my cars because I needed the money to continue paying my bills. I made a decision to sell one of my cars, so I did! I still was going into foreclosure, but there was nothing I can do. I knew that I filled out an application for Save the House, but I hadn't heard anything from them. With my back against the wall, all alone, scared, I still believed in me! I didn't know how it was going to happen, but I'd been counting on me all my life! I didn't get this far to give up now! Yes, I was scared and alone, but I believed in me! That day ended too.

The next day came. I had to go to physical therapy where I did my therapy for my stroke. The social worker was great. Her name was Summer. She helped me fill out lots of paperwork that I needed for the programs I applied for.

Summer said, "Brett, it's June now. Have you heard anything from Save the House?"

I said, "No, but, Summer, my house is going into foreclosure. An attorney sent me a letter saying that my mortgage company has contained them, and they were in the process of beginning the foreclosure proceedings on the property at Pine Street."

Summer asked, "What are you going to do, Brett?"

"Summer, I've been fighting all my life! I'm at a crossroads in my life. I believe that I will get through this. I'm keeping my faith, so at this time, all I can do is wait."

Summer said, "Brett, you have a great attitude! You got most of the battle won with your attitude!"

I said, "Thank you, Summer. I will let you know when I hear something."

"Okay, Brett, have a nice day."

"You too, Summer." Our meeting was over, and the therapy was over. The secretary called for my transportation. They came and took me back home. It was a quiet day for me after therapy. It was like the calm before the storm. I was definitely in the storm!

The next day came, and I got a call from the CC Administration Office. I was excited, but I was nervous at the same time. I had to answer the phone because that's the call I'd been waiting for. I picked up the phone, and a man on the other end said, "Can I speak to Brett Jones?"

"I'm him."

The man introduced himself and said he was an officer at the CC Administration. "By law, I had to call you to let you know that you have been denied CC benefits."

I asked, "Why? I had a stroke."

He said he didn't know. "But you might want to contact an attorney to help you with this situation because you can appeal the decision we made at CC." I said thank you.

I was in shock. It was unbelievable, but I was told by certain friends that you always get denied the first time you apply for CC!

At the time, I kept seeing commercials about attorneys to help people who have been denied CC, so I called one of the attorneys I had on a piece of paper and told them my story, and they said, "We can help you, Mr. Jones." They set up an interview for me at my house.

A representative came out from the attorney's office, and we sat down, and he conducted the interview. It took about a half hour, and he said, "We do this all the time. We can help you get your CC. Brett, you are a typical case for us. You are going to be fine." I thanked him for his encouragement, and he was a professional, and the look in his eyes gave me hope! "Brett, you are going to be okay." Our meeting was over.

After the interview, I was feeling better about my circumstances. I was thinking about my mortgage. I hadn't heard anything from Save the House. I wanted to call them, but I couldn't. I was already in foreclosure proceedings, so I just waited, but I was in good spirits.

It was now the middle of June 2014, and I didn't know how going into foreclosure works. *How much time do I have?* All these thoughts were going through my head. The next day, it was warm outside, so I sat on my porch, enjoying the warm weather. The grass was turning green. The flowers were blooming. The birds were chirping. The skies were blue. I was encouraged, so I went into my house to make a sandwich. The phone started to ring. I picked it up, and a lady on the phone asked, "Can I speak to Brett Jones?" I said, "I'm him."

"My name is Rumia. I'm calling from Save the House, and I have good news for you. Brett, you have been approved for our program!" I was so excited! Rumia said, "Brett, we have set up a time for you to go close on the program. You have to go to a title company in Canal River on June 22, 2014, to sign the paperwork to close on the program. Your appointment time is 10:00 a.m., but be there a little earlier, Brett." Then Rumia started to tell me about the program. She said, "The program will back pay from January 1, 2014, till December 31, 2014, then it would start payment January 1, 2015, all the way through December 31, 2015, and then the program is over for you, Brett. You will have to start paying your mortgage January 1, 2016!" I was so happy. It was like a dream come true! It was unbelievable. It was reality. I was hoping and praying that this would happen over all these months. I was waiting and anticipating, and I was approved! I was so happy!

Then Rumia asked me, "Brett, do you have any question for me?" I told her that I was very thankful that I was approved for the program. "I work as an EMS driver, and I help people with disabilities all over the state, and I am blessed to be approved." I told Rumia I would call her after I have signed the papers.

"Brett, get well."

"Thank you, Rumia." We hung up.

After the call from Save the House, I called my social worker and told her the good news! I told Summer I was approved for the program of Save the House. They would send me out some documents, and I would have to fill them out and take them with me at closing. Summer was so happy for me. It was great after all this time. I was approved. My house is saved! Summer said, "Brett, when you receive your paperwork from Save the House, bring them up, and I will fill them out for you."

"Thank you, Summer. When I receive them, I will call you!"

Summer said, "That's great news for you, Brett." She asked me how I was doing. I said, "Great, Summer, now that I know that I'm approved for the program."

She said, "Brett, I know you are!" So we hung up.

CHAPTER 26

A week later, the papers came from Save the House. I called Summer, the social worker, and she set up the appointment. I went out to her office, and we filled out the paperwork. She called Save the House and asked them, "Would Brett have to pay back this loan?" They said no. "As long as Brett's on the program, he cannot refinance his home, and he cannot sell his home or file for bankruptcy under the circumstances. Brett does not have to pay back the loan: but if he does one of the restrictions, then he will have to pay the loan back in full." Summer said thank you, and she hung up.

Summer looked at me, and she could see that I was relieved. She had been with me all through this process. "Brett, I know you are glad this is over! I can't imagine, Brett, what you have been through, but you seem to be okay through the process."

"Summer, I was concerned because I work hard to keep my home. I had been in my home for twenty-three years. To lose it like this because I had a medical emergency, it would have been heartbreaking for me, Summer, but I believe things would be okay for me."

"Brett, I know you are glad it's all over."

"Yes, I am!"

Now that it was over, I was relieved from worrying about the home I bought for me and my wife and family. I was still in my home, so that made me feel a lot better. I hadn't heard anything from CC yet! The summer was going by pretty fast. A few months went by. It was now September. My birthday was coming up. I'll be fifty-seven years old. I didn't have any plans for my birthday, but I was just thankful that the current events that I just experienced were over! That made me feel a lot better.

September was coming to an end. I had two months of finance left to pay my bills. After that, I'll be broke! I was hoping that I might hear from CC. It's been eight months since I filled out the application back in February for CC. I had been told that it could take up to two years to get CC. I hoped it would come sooner than later.

October came in. Fall was on its way in. It started to get darker earlier. Everything was changing. The colors of the leaves were changing. It was pretty, so I took it a day at a time. October was moving right along. It was the second week of October, and still no word from CC. I hoped it didn't take two years. I had a stroke! I was not asking for a handout! CC was set up for Americans to have something to fall back on just in case they have an emergency. Well, I have a medical emergency. I had a stroke. Why do I have to wait almost a year to get approved for CC?

The third week of October came. I was not thinking about CC anymore. I was mentally exhausted!

During that week, I was thinking about selling my other car because I was running out of money. I didn't want to sell my car, but I didn't have any other choice! I thought, If by the middle of November I haven't heard anything from CC, I have no choice: I have to sell my car! I have to pay my bills. Today is the third Wednesday of October. The month is coming to an end, so I'm just taking it one day at a time.

The next day came. I was eating my lunch, and the phone started ringing. When I looked at my phone, I saw a Chicago number. I was wondering, *Did my friend get a new phone number? The lady that helped me earlier in the year?* I wasn't sure, so I picked up the phone and said hello. A lady said, "Can I speak to Brett Jones?"

"I'm him."

She introduced herself. "I'm Ruth from the CC Administration Office, and by law, we have to call you to let you know you have been approved for the CC Disability Insurance, and you will get your back pay starting November of 2014. You will get your first installment of the CC Disability Insurance payment in December of 2014." Then the lady was telling me about CC and how to go online at CC. She said, "Set up your account and get all the information you need to understand all your benefits, and there's a toll-free number on there, so you can call to speak to a customer care specialist if you have any questions."

Ruth asked me, "Brett, do you have any question for me?"

I said, "Ruth, I have been waiting for this call for eight months! And I'm glad the wait is finally over. Ruth, I was born in Chicago in 1957. How fitting that the state I was born in would be the state that called me to let me know I have been approved for CC. I am very happy, Ruth. I work hard all my life! I work as an EMS service driver and transported all over the state. Ruth, I did good in my life. I'm a homeowner, so I am glad to be approved for CC."

Ruth said, "Sounds like you did a good job for yourself, Brett!"

I said, "Thank you, Ruth, and have a great day!"

"Brett, get well and happy holidays."

"You too, Ruth." We hung up.

CHAPTER 27

At the time, I was seeing a lady. Her name was Aisha. I called her. She was so excited for me because she had told me earlier that her sister was trying to get on CC, and it took her two years to get on it. Before I got the call, I was thinking about what she said about her sister. I was hoping that wasn't the case! Aisha was happy for me because she was helping me. The day was Thursday, and Aisha was at work. She told me, "Brett, I'm coming over to spend the weekend with you. Let's celebrate on your approved CC and have a great weekend! I will cook dinner for you, Brett."

"Thank you, Aisha! I would like that." She had to get back to work, so we hung up, and I was so relieved. I can now start making plans to meet my financial obligations, so going into 2015, I was looking at my bills and which ones to pay off first. I paid off two bills and was working with two other financial institutions to settle with them, so that day ended too.

The next day, I could finally see the light! I can start putting my life back together with the stroke and everything I just went through. It's amazing that I faced all my fears over all these months, and in the end, I still believed that I would be okay! In the end, no matter what I was going through, I was an older guy who had a stroke and wasn't looking for a handout!

Later on that day, Aisha called me and said she was getting off work, and she was on her way over. "I will be looking for you. What time you think you might be here?"

"It's 4:00 p.m. I will see you around 5:30 p.m."

I said, "I'll see you then." We hung up.

Aisha got to my house about 5:15 p.m. She brought some groceries with her for the dinner she said she would cook, and she ordered a pizza. Aisha was very nice to me. I really appreciated her, and we had a great weekend. Aisha left on Sunday about 6:00 p.m. I went on with the rest of my evening, watched some football, and went to bed about 10:00 p.m.

The next day, I started to make plans for New Year!

October ended. Going into November, I was thinking about Thanksgiving dinner and paying my bills going into next year.

Going into the third week of November, I was thinking about what Ruth said about my back pay. I hadn't received it yet, so Monday of that week, I checked my bank account, and my back pay had been posted to my account. I was very happy to start the process of actually paying my bills, so that's what I did!

November came to an end. Going into December, I was thinking about Christmas, but I was also thinking about therapy and all the nice people who helped me in my recovery at physical therapy! I bought chocolate cherries for the therapists who helped me. They were so excited and very happy to see that. I was glad to spread cheer for the Christmas season.

This was the first year for the College Football Playoff! The four teams were Ohio State and Alabama in the Sugar Bowl and Florida State and Oregon in the Rose Bowl. The two teams that win their game play for the First National Championship in the New Playoff Series.

New Year finally came. It was time for the football games. It was exciting: Ohio State Buckeyes #4 vs. Alabama Crimson Tide #1 and Oregon Ducks #2 vs. Florida State Seminoles #3.

Ohio State Buckeyes beat the Alabama Crimson Tide 42–35. The Oregon Ducks beat the Florida State Seminoles 59–20.

Now it was time for the National Championship! Ohio State vs. the Oregon Ducks. The Ohio State Buckeyes beat the Oregon Ducks in the First Playoff Championship Football Game 42–20.

It was exciting to watch the game Go Buck #1.

The New Year came, and I was thinking about the football game and my New Year's resolutions. I was thinking about 2015, and I was so excited that the process of being approved for all the programs was over!

The New Year 2015 was a fresh new start, so for the first six months of 2015, I was checking my mail and watching all my bills and financial statements come in, and seeing where I was, I just went through a tremendous experience recovering from a stroke! As of June 2015, I was getting caught up in my bills. I still had two bills to pay, but I was working on them! I was preparing for the second half of 2015, getting ready for Save the House to expire at the end of the year.

In June of 2015, I received a call from Nikita, my previous employer, and she asked me how I was doing. The phone call caught me by surprise. I said, "I'm fine."

She said, "I have been thinking about you, Brett, and we want you to come to our company. We miss you." As she was saying that, I was thinking, *Why would you ask me that? I came out to your home and told you that they wanted to fire me, and you said, "No one can fire you but me and my brother."* Then I told her thanks for thinking about me and asking to come back to the company.

"Nikita, I can't come back to the company because the company I loved and respected let me down. When I needed the company to support me, the company was not there, like I supported the company. When the company needed drivers, I got the company drivers. Nikita, that hurt me!"

She didn't say anything because she knew that what the company did to me hurt me! She said, "Brett, I can understand. I'm sorry that we let you down. You didn't deserve that, Brett."

I said, "Nikita, I forgive you and the company, and I wish the best for the company."

She said, "Thanks, Brett." We hung up, and that was the last time I talked to Nikita.

In the year 2015, my mother passed away. She never told me that she loved me. She never showed that she cared! I had been in my home for twenty-four years. She called me maybe three times and visited me maybe two times. I just couldn't believe it, but it is what it is. I will never know why my mother disliked me so much. She never told me about my father. I asked her a lot over the years. She was always angry at me, so I got through the passing of my mother, and I was moving forward with my life. She was never in my life, but she loved her other children, my brothers and sisters. I love them, but I had to divorce from them, like I said earlier in my story. It was unbelievable.

I was preparing for 2016, making sure that I was ready to start paying my mortgage starting January 1, 2016. So 2015 was moving fast. It was June, and I was right where I wanted to be. I had two more bills to pay, so I was working on them. A few months went by. It was now September, going into my birthday. My birthday came, and I turned fifty-eight years old. A couple of months passed. The holidays were here. Thanksgiving came. I spent a quiet day at home and cooked a turkey breast and trimmings and watched football. It was an exciting time for me! I was getting ready for Christmas and didn't have a lot of gifts to get this year. I bought a couple of gifts for some good friends, and that was my Christmas of 2015. The New Year was right around the corner, so I was making my New Year's resolution for 2016.

My New Year's resolution for 2016 was the year of learning—that's my theme for the year!

CHAPTER 28

The New Year came, and I was thinking about refinancing my house to pay off all my bills that accumulated while I was waiting to get approved for CC. Two months went by, and I started getting calls from a collection agency about a bill I hadn't paid. I talked to them, and I explained to them, "I had a stroke, and my life has changed. I'm now on a fixed income. I want to work with your agency." I told the agent that I was working on something. "I'm going to try to settle with your agency. Give me a little time. I'm trying to work something out. I think it looks good, but I'm not sure yet, but I will be in touch with your agency."

The agent said, "Thank you. I'll talk to you in about thirty to sixty days." I said thank you, and we hung up.

After talking to the collection agency, I made my mind up to refinance my home. I kept seeing an ad on TV about low rates on refinancing your home, so I called an agency and told them that I liked to take advantage of the low refinance rates. I would like to refinance my home. The agent said, "We can help you with that." We filled out the application, and he said, "We will communicate with you by email. We'll be sending you emails of more documents we need from you to complete the process. It will take about thirty days. We like to close your application in thirty days." I said thank you, and we hung up.

The whole month of March, they were sending me emails saying that they needed certain documents, and that went on throughout March. I supplied all the documents they needed. March ended, and April came in. The first week of April they sent me an email saying that it was time to reappraise my home and that's the final step in the application process, so they set up a date for the appraiser to come out. The second week of April, the appraiser came out, and she said, "Oh, what a nice home you have,

Mr. Jones." I said thank you, so she came into my house, and I told her, "My home is your home." She smiled, and she started to do the appraisal.

"Mr. Jones, you keep a clean house."

"Thank you."

"The only thing I see is that when they look at your basement walls, they might not want to approve you because your walls need to be painted, but I will submit it." I said thank you, and she left.

A week went by. I got a call from the financial institution's appraisal department, and they said my appraisal came in low, $60,000. But when I bought my house in May of 1992, I paid $62,500. I had been in my house for twenty-four years! I was on a $76,000 refinance, and my balance was only $13,900. How could my appraisal come back at $60,000?

On the state's website, the value of my property was $67,000, and I looked at two other websites, and my property value was $72,000.

I felt cheated. I had been seeing people over the years on TV who paid $300,000 for their homes, and now their homes are not worth $200,000, so I get it. Buying a home is the American Dream. It is something to be proud of, to have a property, to have equity in your home, to borrow off your home! I was very disappointed the appraisal didn't go through. I was just very disappointed!

I called the collection agency and told them that I tried to refinance my home, and the appraisal came in low, and I wasn't able to refinance, so I was not in a position to pay my debt. I was on disability—a fixed income! The agent said, "Can you send me proof of what you just said so I can send that to my client?"

I said, "I can. I will fax the information to you." He said great, and we hung up. I faxed the information to him. After that, I was hoping to buy some time because time was my best friend at that moment. I'm on a thirty-year mortgage. My maturity date is 2022, but I'm on a biweekly plan, and I'm saving six years off a thirty-year mortgage. But because I had a stroke, I will save four years, so I called my mortgage company to find out exactly when I would pay my mortgage off. The customer representative lady said, "Mr. Jones, you will pay your mortgage off March of 2018. Congratulations! I know you will be happy to pay your home off! You only have fifteen months left!"

That's why time was my best friend! I was hoping that the collection agency would give me this time given my situation. I had a stroke and now on a fixed income!

A few months went by. It was now August, and I was just looking at my mail, and I saw two letters from an attorney's office. One said that they are representing the financial institution that I wasn't able to pay, and they are taking me to court to sue me for my unpaid debt! I was surprised. This had never happened to me before, and the letter stated that they could confiscate all my possessions. They could put a lien on my house. I really got nervous and scared! I was really nervous, so I opened the second attorney's letter, and it stated that they can help me file Chapter 7 bankruptcy: "Mr. Jones, you only have thirty days before they sue you." I called the attorney's office and gave the representative the reference number that was on the document, and the lady said, "Mr. Jones, you have thirty days before they sue you. We have an appointment open for today at twelve o'clock noon. Can you make it?"

"Yes, I can." She set up the appointment, and I went in at noon and talked to the attorney. He could see that I was nervous, and he said, "Mr. Jones, you can relax. The bankruptcy law was set up for people like you. You had a medical emergency. You were off work. You weren't able to pay your finances. You're a classic case for Chapter 7 bankruptcy." Then the attorney gave me their fee. I looked it over. I had no choice because I cared about my home and everything I worked for all my life! So I agreed to the fee and paid the attorney. He set up an appointment. That day was Saturday. He set the appointment up for Monday of the next week. They weren't wasting any time. They knew the laws, thirty days before I get sued! They told me what they would need at my appointment, and I said thank you and went home. When I got home, I got all the document they needed, and I was ready for my appointment.

When Monday came, I went to my appointment and sat down with two attorneys. They looked at the documents they asked me to bring in, and they said, "Mr. Jones, everything looks good." They started asking me a lot of questions, and I answered them. Then after that, the attorney started telling me about the 341 hearing. I didn't know what a 341 hearing was, and they told me, "The 341 hearing is a meeting of creditors where they ask you questions under oath about your bankruptcy and rule to discharge your debts."

"Oh."

The attorney told me, "You will receive a letter in the mail when your 341 hearing would be held, and, Mr. Jones, you have to be at the 341 hearing or they will throw your case out, and you will have to start all over again and pay the fee again! We don't want that!"

"I will be at my 341 hearing."

The attorneys said, "Brett, by law, you have to take two tests before you go to your 341 hearing. Here's the website. Go home and log on and do your first test, and when you finish the first test, the website will tell you when you have to take the second test before you go to the 341 hearing."

"Okay, I will take both tests before my 341 hearing."

"Okay, Brett, and we will see you there." The meeting was over, and I went home.

I went home and logged on to the website they gave me and took the first test. It took about ninety minutes. I actually liked taking the test. There were a lot of questions about wants and needs, managing your spending habits, do you need it, or do you want it? After I finished the first test, the website told me, "Your next test would be the third week of August, any day that week." The third week of August came, and I took the second test, and it took about sixty minutes. The website stated I should call the Debtor Education Center to be certified so I can get my certificate for taking the test. I called, and they verified that I took the test, and they would send a copy to my attorney. They would send me my certificate through email, and I did receive my certificate, and the test was completed. The last week of August, I received a letter from my attorney's office stating, "Brett, you have your hearing date, which is September 9, 2016, at 10:00 a.m. Be down there, and we will meet you there."

September came in. It was my birthday month. I will be turning fifty-nine years old this month. The ninth of September was here, and I went to my 341 hearing. My attorney met me down there, and we waited till they called my case hearing. After about a half hour to forty-five minutes, they called my case. We went in to the magistrate's courtroom, and the attorney did all the talking, and the magistrate asked me some questions. Then it was over in about fifteen minutes.

When it was over, the attorney told me, "Mr. Jones, the magistrate has granted you a discharge, and in about thirty to sixty days, you will receive an official letter stating that you were granted a discharge, and it would all be over!" She said, "Brett, it's a new fresh start for you! Good luck and get better."

I said, "Thank you!" I left and went home, and I was so relieved!

The next day, I was thinking about all I just went through—all my fears, all the stress I went through, all the nervousness I went through, on the brink of losing my home, going into foreclosure. I was just going through so much since I had my stroke: *The Edge of Dawn: When No One Cared, I Did!* But I'm still here and looking forward to my new life! Now I have time to write out my whole life story, and that's exactly what I'm going to do, because I live an extra-extraordinary life. I don't know how anyone could have done what I did, but I did it, with no help from my family.

My birthday came. I turned fifty-nine years old. I was getting ready for the holidays. The year 2016 was the year of learning for me. It was my theme, and what a year it was! I learned a lot!

Halloween, Thanksgiving, and Christmas came; and I enjoyed all of the holidays. During that time, I was doing a lot of walking. I was enjoying my new life! I just went through the storm! I just went through a tremendous experience in my life!

My New Year's resolution for 2017 was the final countdown—that's my motto for 2017!

Why the final countdown? Because after all I've been through, I will be paying my mortgage off at the end of 2017. I will have three payments left, and I'll be done! It's been a long road. I've been in my home twenty-six years of a thirty-year mortgage. I was on the biweekly plan on my mortgage. I was supposed to save six years off a thirty-year mortgage, but since I had a stroke, I'm saving four years, but I'm still saving after all the adversities I had to go through! I stayed tough, strong, and focused!

So 2017 came in. I always broke the year down into quarters. I wanted to see the first quarter where I was and if I met my projection. The first quarter, I was watching my budget. The second quarter, I was to make sure that I kept all the "repair service programs" that I was on like electrical lines in my home and my hot water heater and my furnace. The third quarter was getting out of the house and starting to do things that I was unable to do before like trimming my trees, washing the siding down on my house that I wasn't able to do the last couple of years because I was recovering from my stroke, and starting to live again. The last quarter was the "final countdown." It's finally here, the last quarter of 2017, less than six months away from paying my home off! What a marvelous and great day that's going to be!

The year 2017 came to an end, and 2018 came in.

My 2018 New Year's resolution" (The Stretch Run/The Breakout Year) is to do something that I have never done before like start my family at sixty years old! I like to have children to pass on my legacy. I never had a chance to have kids in my whole life! In my old life, I was a stepdad! In my new life, I can have my family and my kids! I would like to take an airplane ride, take a ride on a railroad train, explore America, start traveling, get out. That's what I have been waiting for! The final countdown, March of 2018, was here, the "Stretch Run," and I made my last mortgage payment! It's all over. I did it! Congratulations, Brett, you have done it! Your house is yours!

The End

COMMENTARY

$\mathcal{T}$he reason I wrote my story is I think my story is unique. I grew up in the sixties with racial unrest and segregation, desegregation, integration, discrimination, and racial profiling. I grew up watching it all, and there were riots in the streets of America all the time shown on television.

I watched the assassination of John F. Kennedy on television on November 22, 1963, in Dallas, Texas. I was a little boy. A year later, I watched Lyndon B. Johnson sign the Civil Rights Act of 1964. That was a great time for black Americans in America. A year later, in 1965, I watched Lyndon B. Johnson sign the Voting Rights Act for black Americans! During that time, the Vietnam War was going on, and the drafting was in full force. Black Americans at that time were being discriminated and put in jail for nothing. We couldn't sit down at the drugstore lunch counters. When ordering food, we had to go to the back of the store to get our order. At that time, black Americans were segregated from schools. America didn't want black Americans to integrate into their schools. It was one of the worst times for black Americans! Now America is drafting black Americans at a record pace to fight in an unpopular war, the Vietnam War. We are good enough to go to a foreign land and fight and die there, but in our own country, we can't even sit at the lunch store counter or get a good education. At the time, that was the feeling in America! If you read America's black history, this is a fact!

Growing up as a little boy in the sixties wasn't normal!

On April 4, 1968, Martin Luther King Jr. was assassinated in Memphis, Tennessee. At that time, discrimination and racial tension were prevalent. There was unfairness in America. The country exploded from California to Detroit to Chicago to down South. The country was on fire! Riots were in most of American cities. It was a shame America was that prejudiced toward black Americans!

Months later, Robert Kennedy was assassinated, June 5, 1968, in Los Angeles, California.

I was ten years old, going on eleven, when my brothers started going to jail. It was just me and my sister Sue, and then I noticed my mother changed toward me. She started having more children. She had three more kids: Judy, Wanda, and Ben, my sisters and brother.

And that's when my story started, the one you just read!

So, Brett, how did you get through all that? Well, I will tell you. I was a little boy in the sixties growing up with other kids. I was totally dependent on my mother. All the events that I experienced through that decade, that's how it was for me!

Then the seventies came in. My brothers were still in jail! It was just me, my other brother, and my sisters. My mother moved from the Arms up to Moon Street. I was going on twelve years old, going to the seventh grade. I went to Hays Junior High School.

Then my mother bought her new house on Cole Street. She was so happy! I was happy for her! The time was 1972. Integration was a law. I started riding the bus to a school called Smith Junior High School to get a better education! It was an all-Caucasian School. I finished the seventh grade there.

Then 1973 came. I finished eighth grade at Smith Junior High School. That's where I met my first Caucasian girlfriend, Pam.

So 1973 came in. I liked Smith Junior High School. The students got along great. I never had any problem about being black or white. It was great there!

On March 1, 1973, I went to school. We had a math test that day, so we took the test, then school was out. We got on the school bus and went home. We got off the school bus, and we saw the police car parking there. The police officer got out of the car with a guy, and the guy pointed at me and said, "He's the one who snatched the lady's pocketbook." I told the police officer that I just got out of school. "You can come to my mother's house and call the school." He did. The principal told him that Brett was in school all day! So then the police officer said, "Since I have an eyewitness, I have to take you to jail!" The police took me to jail for snatching a lady's pocketbook!

My mother never supported me. She knew that I was innocent! She knew I was in school, but she didn't support me! She didn't fight for her son like a mother should!

That's when I knew my mother didn't care. The court sentenced me to the Department of Youth Services where I did time for a crime I didn't commit.

So I took that negative and turned it into positive. Yeah, I was mad, upset, disappointed in the court, but I spent my time reading books. I wasn't going to let this get me down!

So I got out of jail. I graduated high school in 1977. A week later, my mother called the police on me and kicked me out of her house! I slept in my car for one night and ask a friend mother if could stay at her home till I get my apartment, and at the time, I was driving a cab.

Early in my story, I talked about things I learned while I was incarcerated, like masturbating. There were things in there that I didn't want to be part of. I saw things happen in there. When I was in high school, we had a sex education class about safe sex to help safeguard us from STD and unwanted pregnancies, stuff like that, so it's okay to practice safe sex.

The thing I like about me was I never gave up. I was always positive. That was and still is my outlook. No matter what you have to go through in life, you can do it! You are going to have to make hard decisions like I did. I had to make hard decisions and not break the law. Do not break the law! It is the key!

You are going to have setbacks. You are going to have a hard time in dealing with problems. You are going to have people talk about you and lie on you, spread rumors about you. It's your attitude that's going to help you! Sticks and stones may break my bones, but words will never hurt me. Stay positive. When no one believe in you, believe in yourself because it's all about you, not them.

I have a saying: it's not how fast you reach the top but how fast you pick yourself up when you hit bottom, such as getting fired from work for something you didn't do, people spreading rumors about you, jealousy, your girlfriend cheating on you with your best friend—how will you deal with it? Love is the strongest emotion inside of us. Be careful with it. It can cut like a two-edged sword. Will you go negative and break the law to hurt yourself, or will you stay positive and learn from it to build character?

You see, everything I went through, I stay positive. All the chapters, all the different parts of my life, from being a child to a young teenager to a young adult to being a stepdad and everything else in between, I stay positive!

Brett, how did you do it when you had no family help, no guidance of a father, no mother to love you? Brett, it must have been tough. It was!

Here's how I did it. I kept my mind active! I didn't let depression come in. I didn't let feeling sorry for myself come in. I didn't let loneliness come in. I didn't let anger come in. You have two learn forgiveness, believe in second chances. All of this build character and self-esteem!

I kept my mind active. I worked all the time. I didn't have time to feel sorry for myself. I was always looking forward to the next day!

Keep your mind active! Well, Brett, what do you mean keep your mind active? Always have something to do! Have a plan! Have objectives you like to meet. Look at things quarterly, semiannually, and annually. Always know where you are in your life!

Have empathy. Put yourself in others' shoes. Be transparent and fair! Help someone! Read books to learn how other people solve their problems. You'd be surprised you're not the only person who had to make hard decisions. You can learn a lot! You will have to separate from your friends in your teenage years, usually between sixteen, eighteen, and twenty-five years old to get a part-time job. If you stay with your friends, you lose time. Time is key! Learn time, work in time, stay in time—time is a friend! Time is all we have. Treasure it!

These are your learning years, sixteen through twenty-five years old. You're finding out what you want to do in your life. You're probably getting ready to graduate from high school. What do you want to do? You might want to go into the armed forces and make a career out of the military. Keep your mind active! Always keep options just in case things don't work out. Do you want to go to college? If not, when seeking employment, get a trade: electrician, air conditioning, heating service, repair person, plumber, etc. Do not get a job—get a career! These are some tools to think about that can help you along the way. I wish I knew about these tools when I was growing up. I wish I had a father to tell me this. That's why you have to separate from your friends, so you can concentrate on your future. You might meet a nice girlfriend. You might want to get married and have a family in the future. It is very important to stay focused. Stay in time. Understand who you are and what you want out of life. Look at me. I wanted to start a family at age sixty. See how long it took me to get at this point in my life? It takes *time*! Be patient.

So that's what I mean when I say keep your mind active!

When you get to the fork in the road, which way will you go: left or right? I went right. You see, in the end, it was never about them. It was always about me and the decisions I had to make.

Which way will you go?

Do the right thing!

Believe in yourself!

I have a saying: there are those who want it and those who go out and get it. Which one are you?

Understand balance is everything—right and wrong, left and right, night and day!

Be responsible! It builds character.

Sometimes you will have to learn on your own good or bad.

Sometimes you have to take a stand, a position.

Leave yourself with something to do.

Be patient!

Work in time it your friend!

Be a cheerful loser. Honor life and the game!

Losing keeps you humble!

Take nothing for granted!

Don't be afraid to make a mistake! Learn from it. It's okay. Be afraid if you don't learn from it.

You always get setbacks. Will you be able to bounce back?

Learn how two adapt.

Keep your composure!

Sacrifice time to make time.

Respect yourself. Give yourself a chance. Be a good steward.

Be imaginative. Give yourself options. Imagine all the possibilities.

Have an opinion. These are good tools to have with you on your journey through life.

Remember the three eight' sleep work and life' very important'

Keep good physical hygiene it build confidence' and self-esteem!

Put your footprint on the earth' to keep your legacy alive'

Don't play safe all the time take chances possibility likelihood expectation anticipation'

What are you doing for yourself?

Think before you make a decision!

Keep searching!

Be persistent.

Persevere. Be determined!

Trust your gut. It is always right!

Look up the terms "illusion" and "deception." Don't get caught in them.

Be like a long-distance runner—endure to the end!

Run your life like a business.

Take inventory of yourself: quarterly, semiannually, and annually.

See if you're coming close to your projections.

Make the decision!

Learn sacrifice!

Discover discipline!

Be vibrant!

Grow into maturity!

Talk to yourself!

Listen to yourself!

When people abandon you, don't abandon yourself!

Anything worthwhile takes time!

Find your passion, and go with your heart!

Read books!

Look up the word "adversity"!

Look up the word "restraint"!

A gesture of good is good everywhere!

Learn the rules of engagement! Otherwise, learn the rules of life, the dos and the don'ts, the right thing and the wrong thing. Which one will you do? Make the decision!

You see, in the end, it was never about them! It was always about you!

Good luck. Have fun along the way. Hold on to something tight, and enjoy the journey of life!

You can do it!

www.ingramcontent.com/pod-product-compliance
Lightning Source LLC
Chambersburg PA
CBHW071008120626
46546CB00003B/990